T0324133

American Justice 2019

Garrett Epps, Consulting Editor

American Justice 2019
The Roberts Court Arrives

Mark Joseph Stern

PENN

UNIVERSITY OF PENNSYLVANIA PRESS

PHILADELPHIA

Copyright © 2019 University of Pennsylvania Press

All rights reserved. Except for brief quotations used for purposes of review or scholarly citation, none of this book may be reproduced in any form by any means without written permission from the publisher.

Published by
University of Pennsylvania Press
Philadelphia, Pennsylvania 19104-4112
www.upenn.edu/pennpress

Printed in the United States of America

A Cataloging-in-Publication record is available from the Library of Congress

Cover design by John Hubbard

ISBN 978-0-8122-5213-2

Contents

Introduction

The Chief Takes Charge

On the morning of October 9, 2018, the justices of the U.S. Supreme Court walked from behind the red velvet curtains in the courtroom and took their seats on the bench. The arguments that day were relatively dull—they all involved complex questions about a sentencing enhancement law—but the courtroom was electric. Outside, crowd-control barricades blocked access to the gleaming white marble front plaza. On the concrete sidewalk in front of the building, a small cluster of women in blood-red costumes featured in the TV show *The Handmaid's Tale* held signs in silent protest. "We the people do not consent," one read. "Happy first day, liar," said another. Court police kept watch from the plaza, warily eyeing the protesters. A gray sky hung low over the marble palace, adding to the subdued mood of the demonstration.

Eight days earlier, the court opened the new term—formally called the October 2018 term, or O.T. 2018—with only eight members. The U.S. Senate was embroiled in a heated debate over the confirmation of then-nominee Brett Kavanaugh. On October 6, the Senate confirmed

Kavanaugh by a razor-thin margin. Just hours later as swarms of furious protestors pounded on the court's massive bronze doors, Justice Kavanaugh was sworn in.

October 9 marked Kavanaugh's debut on the bench. Before beginning the day's proceedings, Chief Justice John Roberts made a brief announcement. "Before we commence the business of the court this morning," Roberts said, "it gives me great pleasure, on behalf of myself and my colleagues, to welcome Justice Kavanaugh to the court." Then the chief justice admitted attorneys to the Supreme Court bar, a routine that precedes oral arguments. As he spoke, Kavanaugh interacted with Justice Elena Kagan, who sits to his right. The two chatted and laughed like old friends. For the rest of the morning, there was no clue that anything was out of the ordinary except the absence of seats in the back of the courtroom—the wooden chairs on which spectators from the public typically sit for a brief glimpse of the justices in action. It seemed that the court had limited public attendance to minimize the risk that protesters might interrupt the newest justice's first arguments.

Kavanaugh's appearance on the bench marked the end of one of the most astonishing and painful chapters in the court's history. President Donald Trump nominated him on July 9 to replace Justice Anthony Kennedy, the court's perennial swing vote. For years, Kennedy had frustrated conservatives by periodically siding with the four liberal justices on contentious issues, including abortion, same-sex marriage, and capital punishment. Kavanaugh, a former Kennedy clerk, evinced no interest in filling his old boss's shoes as a swing vote. His career was steeped in Republican politics: He had aided Kenneth Starr's investigation into President Bill Clinton, worked for George

W. Bush during the Florida recount, and served as White House staff secretary during the Bush administration. In 2006 Kavanaugh was confirmed to the U.S. Court of Appeals for the District of Columbia Circuit, where he served as an ardent conservative. The replacement of Kennedy with Kavanaugh was bound to be controversial. Liberals were still livid that Senate Republicans had refused to consider President Barack Obama's nominee, the moderate judge Merrick Garland, after Justice Antonin Scalia died in 2016. Trump had instead placed Justice Neil Gorsuch, a rock-ribbed conservative, in Scalia's seat. Kennedy had appeared to be the one justice standing between the court's four Republican appointees and a conservative revolution in American jurisprudence. Kavanaugh, Democrats feared, would provide the fifth vote to overturn progressive precedent and push the law far rightward. During his initial confirmation hearings in September Kavanaugh was cagey about his views, but his forceful opinions on the D.C. Circuit spoke for themselves. He reliably rejected the legal philosophies that lay behind landmark Supreme Court decisions cherished by the Left. As a judge, Kavanaugh was no centrist.

A bare majority of senators were poised to confirm Kavanaugh when, in September, a psychology professor named Christine Blasey Ford publicly accused him of sexual assault. Ford alleged that in 1982 when she was fifteen and Kavanaugh was seventeen, he and a friend had tried to rape her at a house party. The Senate Judiciary Committee held additional hearings on September 27, 2018, to evaluate the claim. The nation was riveted; more than 20 million people watched on TV. Ford testified about her memory of the night in question with harrowing force and emotion. "I am here today not because I want to be," she told the committee. "I am terrified. I am here because I believe it is my civic duty to tell you what happened to me while Brett Kavanaugh and I were in high school."

Ford said she had no doubt that the man now nominated to the highest court in the land was the same person who thirty-six years earlier had sexually assaulted her. "Brett groped me and tried to take off my clothes," she testified. "He had a hard time because he was so drunk, and because I was wearing a one-piece bathing suit under my clothes. I believed he was going to rape me. I tried to yell for help. When I did, Brett put his hand over my mouth to stop me from screaming. This was what terrified me the most, and has had the most lasting impact on my life. It was hard for me to breathe, and I thought that Brett was accidentally going to kill me."

Kavanaugh then provided impassioned testimony of his own. His voice trembling, his eyes welling with tears, he accused the Democratic senators sitting before him of engaging in a "grotesque and coordinated character assassination." He spoke with raw anger, indignation, and disgust. The Democrats' "well-funded effort to destroy my good name and destroy my family," Kavanaugh declared, was a "calculated and orchestrated political hit, fueled with apparent pent-up anger about President Trump and the 2016 election, fear that has been unfairly stoked about my judicial record, revenge on behalf of the Clintons and millions of dollars in money from outside left-wing opposition groups."

"You sowed the wind for decades to come," he told the senators. "I fear that the whole country will reap the whirlwind."

The Senate's investigation into Ford's allegations shed little light on the truth, as did the Federal Bureau of Investigation's supplemental investigation, upon which the White House imposed strict limitations. In the end, Kavanaugh's emotional testimony carried the day. Every Republican senator except Alaska's Lisa Murkowski supported his confirmation, while every Democratic senator except West Virginia's Joe Manchin came out in opposition. Kavanaugh was confirmed by a vote of 50–48.

Kavanaugh hit the ground running. During his first term, the justice heard two bona fide blockbusters: a constitutional challenge to partisan gerrymandering and an effort to keep a citizenship question off the 2020 census. He also participated in cases involving capital punishment, religious liberty, abortion, criminal justice, workers' rights, antitrust, immigration, trans rights, and the administrative state. In every 5–4 decision but one, Kavanaugh sided with the conservative bloc.

And yet, the Supreme Court term that began in October 2018 was by no means a conservative revolution—thanks in large part to the chief justice. Roberts voted with the liberal justices in several high-profile cases, including the census dispute. He joined the progressive bloc just frequently enough to create the impression that the court had not changed much since Kennedy's retirement. For the most part the justices stayed out of the news, just as Roberts prefers it. Although the end of the term coincided with the first presidential debates among 2020 Democratic hopefuls, no candidate mentioned the court even once. Perhaps the most explosive news story of the past year, Kavanaugh's confirmation, had faded into the political background.

But even as Roberts played the role of centrist, he laid the groundwork for a coming turn to the right. His conservative rulings were sweeping and momentous, such as when he permanently shut out partisan gerrymandering claims from the federal court system. Meanwhile, his ostensibly liberal decisions were extremely narrow, such as when he held that the Trump administration had justified the census citizenship question with unlawful pretext. Several 5–4 rulings weakened the doctrine of stare decisis, or respect for precedent, as the majority diminished its responsibility to adhere to earlier progressive decisions. Roberts kept the court out of the spotlight as the Kavanaugh controversy died down but did not abandon his fundamentally conservative principles.

This book will chart a number of major cases that the U.S. Supreme Court confronted during Kavanaugh's first term. In the process, the text will identify several themes that emerged by the time the justices issued their final opinions on June 27, 2019. To see how the court did not change this term, it is helpful to understand its recent history as well as the role it plays in America's constitutional order.

Article III of the U.S. Constitution vests the "judicial power" in "one Supreme Court" whose justices serve "during good behavior"—that is, for life unless they are impeached and removed. The court may hear only "cases" or "controversies." It cannot issue advisory opinions; for instance, the president cannot ask the justices if a future executive order would be unlawful. Rather, the court must hear real disputes brought by parties with genuine legal injuries. The court mostly hears appeals from "inferior courts"—state supreme courts as well as federal district and appeals courts—and typically gets to choose which cases to take.

The Supreme Court interprets federal law, providing the definitive meaning of congressional statutes. The court also applies the Constitution in regard to the federal government and state governments. Thus, when a certain law, state or federal, violates the Constitution, the Supreme Court must strike it down. Because of this expansive authority, the Supreme Court plays a huge role in American life and politics. The court has enshrined rights to abortion (1973's *Roe v. Wade*), same-sex marriage (2015's *Obergefell v. Hodges*), and keeping a handgun in the home for self-defense (2008's *District of Columbia v. Heller*). In the realm of criminal law, the court has guaranteed criminal defendants the right to an attorney (1963's *Gideon v. Wainwright*) and the right to be advised of their rights upon arrest (1966's *Miranda v. Arizona*), outlawed the execution of the mentally disabled (2002's *Atkins v. Virginia*) and juvenile offenders (2005's *Roper v. Simmons*), and safeguarded the right of individuals to burn an American flag (1989's *Texas v. Johnson*). Regarding racial equality, the court has prohibited the racial segregation of public schools (1954's *Brown v. Board of Education*) as well as the race-based desegregation of public schools (2007's *Parents Involved v. Seattle*). In addition, the court has effectively chosen a president (2000's *Bush v. Gore*) and safeguarded the right of corporations to spend unlimited money on elections (2010's *Citizens United v. FEC*).

This smattering of landmark decisions is just the tip of the iceberg. The Supreme Court has reached into nearly every aspect of American life and injected the judiciary into the hot-button political issues of the day. Under Chief

Justice Earl Warren's tenure from 1953 to 1969, the court moved to the left on civil liberties—particularly race, free speech, and criminal justice—before snapping back to the right under Chief Justice Warren Burger. Yet a series of swing justices have largely prevented the court from moving too far out of step with public opinion. In interpreting the Constitution's majestic generalities, the court has hewn fairly close to the views of most Americans.

Is it healthy in a democracy for so many important issues to be settled by nine lawyers in Washington, D.C.? Few liberals or conservatives are especially consistent here. When the court invalidates a Republican-backed law—say, an abortion restriction—liberals tend to cheer, while conservative tend to complain of overreach. When the court invalidates a Democratic-backed law—say, a handgun ban—conservative tend to cheer, while liberals tend to complain of overreach. The justices too take a contradictory stance toward the court's duties. When they wish to uphold a law, they preach judicial restraint. When they seek to strike one down, they cite their responsibility to enforce the Constitution.

The current chief justice is obviously torn between the competing impulses of conservative ideology and judicial modesty. During his confirmation hearings, Roberts famously said that he would merely "call balls and strikes." On the court, he has joined or authored broad 5–4 decisions that thrust the judiciary even further into the democratic process. He signed onto *Citizens United*, overturning decades of precedent restricting corporation electioneering, and *Heller*, creating an individual right to bear arms. And he authored 2013's *Shelby County v. Holder*, striking down a key provision of the Voting Rights

Act that forced historically racist states to obtain federal approval before altering their voting laws. *Shelby County* invalidated a forty-eight-year-old provision that had just been reauthorized by Congress in 2006. The provision was based on a theory of "equal sovereignty" among states that appears nowhere in the text of the Constitution. Whatever judicial restraint looks like, this was not it.

And yet, when Roberts finds himself in the minority, he accuses his colleagues of judicial activism. In his *Obergefell* dissent, he condemned the court for establishing a constitutional right to same-sex marriage. "The majority's decision is an act of will, not legal judgment," he wrote, and "omits even a pretense of humility." It may be "tempting for judges to confuse our own preferences with the requirements of the law," Roberts concluded. But the Constitution does not allow "five lawyers" to "redefine marriage." Hence his pointed rhetorical question: "Just who do we think we are?"

The difference between *Shelby County* and *Obergefell* came down to one vote: Kennedy. Unlike his colleagues, Kennedy never proclaimed any allegiance to judicial modesty. When he felt that the Constitution required it, he swung far to the right (as in *Shelby County*) or to the left (as in *Obergefell*). His shifting votes forced the remaining justices to continually recalibrate their own attitudes toward the court's proper role in American governance.

Kennedy's departure leaves Roberts as the court's closest approximation to a swing vote. By custom, the Supreme Court informally takes on the name of the chief justice, hence the Warren Court, the Burger Court, and so on. But until Kennedy's retirement, calling the highest court the "Roberts Court" was inapt. For all intents and purposes it was the Kennedy Court, controlled by the man in the middle.* The swing justice's replacement with Kavanaugh, a staunch conservative, marks the true arrival of the Roberts Court. After thirteen years on the Supreme Court, the chief justice finally took control.

The central topic of this book, then, is how Roberts wielded his newfound power. He did not become a moderate or a traditional swing vote; more often than not, he allied with his fellow Republican appointees. In several pitched battles with the Trump administration, however, the chief justice preserved the court's independence in the face of immense pressure from the president.

Roberts's attempt to preserve the U.S. Supreme Court's legitimacy is not the only story of the term. Far from it. Every member of the court strived to shape the law— including Kavanaugh, who wasted no time in making his mark. Difficult cases filled the court's docket and provoked a biting war of words between the justices. The liberal and conservative wings sparred over matters of life and death. Behind-the-scenes drama spilled over into public view.

The chief justice routinely defends the court as a collegial workplace high above the partisan rancor of the day. But this term demonstrated that the Roberts Court is just as deeply divided as the country it serves.

---

* See the discussion in Todd Ruger, *American Justice 2018: The Shifting Supreme Court* (Philadelphia: University of Pennsylvania Press, 2018), 1–12.

Chapter 1

Death Matters

Domineque Ray was prepared to die, with one caveat: he wanted his imam by his side when the moment came. Sentenced to death by an Alabama jury in 1999 for the rape and murder of a teenage girl, Ray converted to Islam behind bars. He was by all accounts a devout practitioner of the faith. But the prison where he sat on death row for thirty years, Alabama's Holman Correctional Facility, provided only a *Christian* chaplain in the execution chamber to comfort inmates as they died. When Ray learned of this policy he sought an accommodation, asking the prison to let his imam accompany him instead. The prison refused, telling Ray his options were a Christian chaplain or nothing.

Five days later, Ray filed a lawsuit alleging a violation of his rights under federal law and the U.S. Constitution. By doing so, he set in motion a chain of events that would lead the justices of the U.S. Supreme Court to feud, bitterly and publicly, about capital punishment and religious liberty. This squabble consumed the court across four separate cases, dividing the justices into warring camps over the jurisprudence of death.

11

Chapter 1

By the time Ray's case landed at the Supreme Court, he had received a reprieve: the U.S. Court of Appeals for the Eleventh Circuit stayed his execution, finding a probable violation of his constitutional rights. On the night of February 7, however, the Supreme Court's conservative bloc reversed the Eleventh Circuit in an unsigned one-paragraph order. The majority alleged that Ray had waited too long to file his lawsuit, forfeiting his ability to litigate Alabama's policy. The Supreme Court allowed his execution to move forward, and he was administered a lethal injection shortly thereafter.

In response, Justice Elena Kagan penned an outraged dissent joined by her liberal colleagues. The majority's decision, she wrote, was "profoundly wrong." Kagan explained that Alabama's chaplain-only policy likely ran afoul of the First Amendment's Establishment Clause, which bars the government from "respecting an establishment of religion." The Supreme Court has held that the "clearest command of the Establishment Clause is that one religious denomination cannot be officially preferred over another." But, Kagan wrote, "the State's policy does just that. Under that policy, a Christian prisoner may have a minister of his own faith accompany him into the execution chamber to say his last rites. But if an inmate practices a different religion—whether Islam, Judaism, or any other—he may not die with a minister of his own faith by his side."

Kagan also noted that Ray hadn't actually filed his lawsuit at the "last minute," as the majority claimed. In reality, Alabama law states that an inmate's spiritual adviser of choice "may be present at an execution." Unbeknownst to Ray, his prison had a secret regulation that distinguishes between advisers who can be in the death chamber (a

Christian chaplain) and those who can watch from the viewing room (everyone else). But the prison "refused to give Ray a copy of its own practices and procedures" laying out this rule. So, he could not have known that his imam would be excluded until he asked, about two weeks before his execution. And just five days after he learned of the rule, he filed his lawsuit. How is that "last minute"?

By the time many court watchers read Kagan's dissent the next morning, Ray had been executed. She lost the battle, but the high court's internal war over Domineque Ray was just beginning. The majority's late-night order drew widespread condemnation from both progressives and conservatives. Describing Ray's imam-free execution as a "grave injustice," *National Review*'s David French scorned the majority for failing to respect the First Amendment's protections "at the moment of his death." Liberal critics such as Amir H. Ali of the MacArthur Justice Center pointed out that the decision was especially troubling in light of the Supreme Court's 2018 decision upholding President Donald Trump's executive order banning travel to the United States from several Muslim-majority countries. "If that was a gut punch to the Muslim community," Ali told the *Washington Post*, "this will be seen as a follow-up kidney shot."

Kagan didn't accuse the majority of anti-Muslim hypocrisy. But she hit them where it hurts. The Supreme Court's conservatives pride themselves on their self-proclaimed solicitude toward religious liberty. In 2014's *Greece v. Galloway*, they allowed a town board to continue opening its meetings with almost exclusively Christian prayers. That same year in *Burwell v. Hobby Lobby*, the conservatives blocked President Barack Obama's administration from applying the contraceptive mandate to for-profit corporations whose Christian owners oppose birth control, citing a federal law protecting religious freedom. In 2018's *Masterpiece Cakeshop v. Colorado Civil Rights Commission*, they held that government officials had expressed impermissible animus when penalizing a Christian baker for turning away a same-sex couple.

True, the court had occasionally ruled in favor of Muslims too, protecting their rights to grow beards in prison (2015's *Holt v. Hobbs*) and wear a headscarf at work (2015's *EEOC v. Abercrombie*). But the court's 5–4 decision in 2018's *Trump v. Hawaii*—upholding the president's travel ban in the face of evidence that he intended it to function as a "Muslim ban"—was still fresh. Now a Muslim inmate was requesting a fairly minor accommodation, and the majority turned him away. Do the conservative justices simply care more about Christians than Muslims and other religious minorities?

The next month, it appeared that this grisly drama was bound to repeat itself. That March a second case with similar facts, *Murphy v. Coller*, made its way to the court: Texas planned to execute Patrick Henry Murphy, a Buddhist. The state provided either a Christian or a Muslim spiritual adviser to inmates in the execution room but refused to let Murphy bring his Buddhist adviser into the death chamber. Murphy, like Ray before him, asked the Supreme Court to block his lethal injection due to this unequal treatment of minority faiths. Pretty much everyone expected the court's conservative justices to turn him away, but they did not.

The *Ray* majority fractured: Justice Brett Kavanaugh peeled off, voting with the liberals to stay Murphy's execution. "In my view," Kavanaugh wrote, "the Constitution prohibits [the] denominational discrimination" that Texas wished to impose. In order to remedy this violation, the state must either allow Murphy's adviser to enter the execution chamber or prohibit *all* spiritual advisers from comforting inmates in their final moments. A few days later Texas issued a new rule taking up Kavanaugh's second offer, denying all inmates access to clergy in the death chamber.

Why did Kavanaugh spare Murphy but not Ray? In a footnote, Kavanaugh wrote that Murphy (unlike Ray) had challenged his prison's policy in "a sufficiently timely manner." But that cannot be right. If anything, Murphy waited much longer than Ray. Recall that Ray didn't learn about Alabama's (secret) policy until about two weeks before his scheduled execution. Murphy, by contrast, had notice of Texas's (public) regulation since at least 2012, when it was first issued. The simplest explanation for Kavanaugh's sudden swing left in *Murphy*, then, is that he changed his mind following the crush of bipartisan criticism that greeted the court's decision in *Ray*.

This didn't mean, though, that Kavanaugh or the other conservatives had formally retreated from their vote in *Ray* and embraced Kagan's dissent—quite the opposite. Four days after Kavanaugh's flip in *Murphy*, he joined an opinion doubling down on *Ray*.

That opinion—the third skirmish in this ongoing battle—was *Bucklew v. Precythe*, a death penalty case that, on the surface, had nothing to do with *Ray* or *Murphy*. It was not about religion but instead was about pain. Missouri planned to execute Russell Bucklew using lethal injection, but he asserted that this method of death would constitute "cruel and unusual punishment" in violation of the Eighth Amendment. Bucklew suffered from cavernous hemangioma, a rare medical condition that covered his neck, throat, lips, and uvula with large blood-filled tumors. A medical expert testified that a lethal injection would cause these fragile tumors to rupture and fill his mouth with blood, leading him to suffocate to death in horrific pain. Bucklew therefore proposed death by nitrogen gas, which was authorized by state law but had not yet been implemented.

This case provided another early test of Justice Brett Kavanaugh's approach to capital punishment. Kavanaugh's predecessor, Justice Anthony Kennedy, had voted to block Bucklew's execution in 2018—a 5–4 decision from which the remaining conservatives dissented. Kennedy obviously believed that Bucklew had presented a serious Eighth Amendment claim. Would his successor agree? He would not.

Days after his liberal vote in *Murphy*, Kavanaugh joined with his fellow conservatives to let Missouri execute Bucklew by lethal injection. And Justice Neil Gorsuch's opinion for the court treated his claims with startling indifference, surveying the history of executions in America as if to say that Bucklew was lucky he didn't face an even more gruesome demise. So long as the state's method of execution does not inflict "gratuitous" pain, Gorsuch wrote, it is constitutional. And because Missouri did not intend to make Bucklew's death unnecessarily painful, it could execute him by lethal injection.

This holding marked a radical shift in Eighth Amendment jurisprudence. Gorsuch's test—forcing death row inmates to prove that the state intended to add gratuitous agony—had never before gained majority support. It was favored by Justices Antonin Scalia and Clarence Thomas, but Kennedy never signed onto it. Here, then, is an instance where Kavanaugh's elevation to the court made a marked difference. His vote allowed Gorsuch to crack down on challenges to executions, imposing a standard that few if any inmates will ever meet.

In *Bucklew*, Gorsuch didn't just change the court's interpretation of the Eighth Amendment. He also seized the opportunity to respond to Kagan's dissent in *Ray*. In an extraneous section at the end of his opinion, Gorsuch wrote that "last-minute" stays of execution "should be the extreme exception," meaning the courts should almost never block executions in the days or hours before they're scheduled to occur. He implied that attorneys for capital inmates were gaming the system, clogging up dockets with frivolous claims just to keep their clients alive. As an example he cited *Ray*, suggesting that Domineque Ray had waited "until just 10 days before his scheduled execution" to file his lawsuit merely so he could avoid imminent death.

In separate dissents, Justices Stephen Breyer and Sonia Sotomayor both wrote rejoinders to Gorsuch's assertion. Breyer reiterated that Ray "brought his claim only five days after he was notified of the policy he sought to challenge" and "raised a serious constitutional question." And Sotomayor tore into Gorsuch's "belated explanation" of the *Ray* decision, debunking his "mistaken premise that Domineque Ray could have figured out sooner that Alabama planned to deny his imam access to the execution chamber." This "skewed view of the facts" led the majority to "misuse" its powers and let Alabama kill Ray.

Once *Bucklew* came down, it seemed that both sides of the debate had aired their grievances and moved on. The conservatives felt certain that they had done the right thing in *Ray*; the liberals were convinced that their colleagues had erred disastrously. Kavanaugh had staked out a middle ground in *Murphy*, crafting a Kennedy-esque compromise. Case closed? Not even close.

On May 13—well over two months after the stay in *Murphy*—Justice Samuel Alito issued a dissent responding to Kavanaugh's concurrence in that case *and* Kagan's dissent in *Ray*. This move was, to say the least, unusual. Opinions relating to these kinds of orders are typically released all at once when they are relevant.

But Alito, it turns out, had fumed for weeks over the events in *Murphy* and *Ray* and chose to release a fourteen-page opinion well after the fact rebutting Kavanaugh and Kagan. The court's decision to stay Murphy's execution, Alito wrote, was "seriously wrong" because prisons have a preeminent interest "in tightly controlling access to an execution room"—one that may apparently outweigh the constitutional guarantee of religious liberty. Besides, Murphy "egregiously delayed in raising his claims," deploying underhanded "tactics" to spare his life. Those "tactics" were "just as unjustified" as Ray's, and the court should have let both men die.

Gorsuch and Justice Clarence Thomas joined Alito's opinion. Incredibly, Kavanaugh decided to respond to Alito, as if trapped in a never-ending game of phone tag with human lives in the balance. Joined by Chief Justice John Roberts, Kavanaugh pointed out that to comply with Alito's *Murphy* concurrence, Texas barred all spiritual advisers from the execution chamber. Thus, his opinion "facilitat[ed] a prompt fix to the religious equality problem in Texas' execution protocol," and this "resolution" should "alleviate any future litigation delays or disruptions."

Then as if to defend his split vote in *Murphy* and *Ray*, Kavanaugh reiterated his (incorrect) belief that Ray waited too long to sue, while Murphy did not. And Kavanaugh wrote that Ray had not presented a First Amendment "equal-treatment argument" as explicitly as Murphy had, if at all. Kavanaugh concluded by reminding "counsel for inmates facing execution" to "raise any potentially meritorious claims in a timely manner." In other words, don't expect Kavanaugh to swing left on any future "last-minute" requests to stay an execution.

What does this contretemps tell us about the post-Kennedy court's approach to death? The main takeaway here is that the conservative justices are tired of dramatic appeals from death row inmates facing the needle in a matter of hours. With Kennedy on the court these appeals stood some chance of success, as he would sometimes spare prisoners while the court mulled their claims. If we take Kavanaugh at his word, those days are over. The new conservative majority thinks that these appeals are part of what Alito once described as "a guerilla war against the death penalty," wherein opponents of capital punishment use every tool at their disposal to gunk up the machinery of death. And the conservative justices will not reward this putative crusade with stays of execution.

These justices made that much clear in the term's fourth and last death penalty skirmish, *Dunn v. Price*. Christopher Lee Price, another Alabama death row inmate, asked the Supreme Court to block his impending execution because the state planned to use midazolam. That drug is supposed to render inmates unconscious before they are injected with chemicals that paralyze them then stop their heart. But some inmates have stayed conscious after they were given midazolam, leading to excruciatingly painful botched lethal injections. Price asked to be killed by nitrogen gas instead. The conservative majority rejected his appeal, alleging that he hadn't filed his claim quickly enough.

In response, Justice Stephen Breyer issued an extraordinary dissent that pulled the curtain back to reveal the magnitude of the inner turmoil at the court. He disclosed that he had asked his colleagues to "take no action until tomorrow, when the matter could be discussed at Conference." They refused, "preventing full discussion among the Court's Members." (This disclosure was a shocking departure from protocol, as the justices never divulge information about their secretive conferences.)

"Should anyone doubt that death sentences in the United States can be carried out in an arbitrary way," Breyer wrote, "let that person review the following circumstances as they have been presented to our Court this evening."

A full month later in an attachment to orders unrelated to the court's decision in *Price*, Thomas issued a retort joined by Alito and Gorsuch. (Again, it is acutely odd for a justice to release an opinion so long after the initial order came down.) In it, Thomas all but accused Breyer of lying. Thomas asserted that Price's only goal was "to delay his execution," and the justice expressed disgust that "four Members of the Court would have countenanced his tactics without a shred of legal support." And Thomas admonished Breyer for supporting these "tactics" by writing a dissent that prevented the court from denying Price's appeal until the middle of the night—after Alabama's execution warrant had expired. The dissent, Thomas wrote, "got its way by default."

On May 30, Price once again asked the court to block his execution. This time, the court turned him away before his execution warrant expired. The vote, once again, was 5–4, and Breyer wrote another short dissent repeating his objections. Alabama promptly executed Price. It appears possible that as Price feared, midazolam did not put him fully to sleep. During the execution he blinked, raised his head, coughed, heaved, and clenched his fist—well after he should have been unconscious.

There is a second lesson to be taken away from all this: Despite the conservatives' all-in approach to *Bucklew*, Kavanaugh and Roberts do not want to be reviled as callous, bigoted, or bloodthirsty. Kavanaugh, after all, may well have buckled under the backlash to *Ray*, and Roberts joined his measured response to Alito's poison-pen letter. Moreover, in February Roberts joined the liberal justices in *Madison v. Alabama*, holding that states may not execute prisoners who do not understand their punishments due to disorders such as dementia. (The decision was 5–3; Kavanaugh did not participate because he had not yet joined the court when *Madison* was argued.) Roberts was willing to play the moderate in this bleak case, preventing Alabama from executing a severely disabled old man.

There is, then, a fault line within the conservative bloc, with Kavanaugh and Roberts unwilling to embrace the extremism of Thomas, Alito, and Gorsuch on matters of death. But it is, at most, a small fissure. In capital cases, the new majority is generally willing to push the law rightward, racing past the limits of Kennedy's wobbly Eighth Amendment jurisprudence while scolding the liberal justices for their impassioned (if futile) dissents. Few may experience the consequences of Kavanaugh's confirmation as painfully as America's death row inmates.

Chapter 2

The Establishment Reversal

Cases involving religion almost always inflame tensions at the U.S. Supreme Court, and adding the death penalty to the mix is a recipe for a conflagration. But O.T. 2018's other big establishment clause dispute, *American Legion v. American Humanist Association*, resulted in a surprisingly harmonious 7–2 decision. The lopsided outcome nevertheless concealed simmering disagreements within the court over state support for religion that will likely boil over in the next term. Where a clash of church and state is concerned, no truce lasts very long at the Supreme Court.

American Legion centers around the massive Peace Cross in Bladensburg, Maryland, only five miles from the Supreme Court Building. If any justices took a field trip across the Anacostia River to visit, they would have instantly seen why the cross became a matter of controversy. The forty-foot-tall concrete cross sits on public land in the median of a three-way juncture on a busy highway. The cross, awash in floodlights by night, towers over everything nearby and is maintained with taxpayer money. Completed in 1925, the Peace Cross was designed as a tribute to forty-nine Maryland soldiers who died in World War I. At its dedication ceremony a Catholic priest gave an invocation, and a Baptist pastor provided a benediction. State representatives encouraged attendees to see the monument as "symbolic of Calvary."

In 2012, a group of secular humanists filed a lawsuit alleging that the cross promoted Christianity in violation of the First Amendment's establishment clause. An appeals court agreed in 2017. Applying the *Lemon* test, the court found that the cross illegally advanced Christianity and fostered excessive entanglement between church and state. The court thus ordered Maryland to alter the cross, relocate it, or transfer its ownership to a private party.

This Supreme Court was never going to let that ruling stand. Its conservative bloc is quite tolerant of religion in public life, even when the government seems to be favoring one religion (usually Christianity) above all others. The real fight in *American Legion*, then, wasn't really about whether the Bladensburg cross would stay or go. It was whether the majority would go for broke by overturning decades of precedent—and specifically the *Lemon* test itself.

To survive this test, a government action must satisfy three prongs: it must have a secular purpose, must not advance or inhibit religion, and must not foster excessive entanglement between religion and government. The test grew out of 1971's *Lemon v. Kurtzman*, in which the court struck down a state law that reimbursed parochial schools for teachers' salaries. Ironically, *Lemon* test was devised by Chief Justice Warren Burger, a conservative who often ruled against church-state separation.

Few legal standards have been subject to more scorn than the *Lemon* test. Like "some ghoul in a late-night horror movie that repeatedly sits up in its grave and shuffles abroad after being repeatedly killed and buried," Justice Antonin Scalia once wrote, "*Lemon* stalks our Establishment Clause jurisprudence." He continued: "The secret of the *Lemon* test's survival, I think, is that it is so easy to kill. It is there to scare us (and our audience) when we wish it to do so, but we can command it to return to the tomb at will." Scalia was echoing a chorus of complaints from conservative jurists and academics who find the test at once too stringent and too malleable.

The *Lemon* test has been sitting in its tomb for quite some time now. While it remains a bête noire of right-leaning commentators, the Supreme Court has not cited it favorably since 2005's *McCreary County v. ACLU*. In that 5–4 decision, the court ordered two Kentucky counties to remove two large copies of the Ten Commandments from their courthouse grounds. The counties had asked the justices to overrule *Lemon*, but the court declined, instead ruling that the monuments had the impermissible purpose of endorsing religion. To detractors such as Scalia, *McCreary County* illustrated everything that is wrong with the *Lemon* test: it lets "the dictatorship of a shifting Supreme Court majority" mandate what he derided as "secularization," excluding religion from "the public forum."

Justice Sandra Day O'Connor cast the fifth vote in *McCreary County*—and retired the next year. Her replacement, Justice Samuel Alito, had consistently voted against establishment clause claims as a judge on the federal court of appeals. In 1999 as a federal judge he wrote a Scalia-esque opinion allowing Jersey City to erect a Nativity scene and a menorah on government property.

Justice Anthony Kennedy dissented in *McCreary County* and other decisions limiting public displays of religious symbols. In fact, Kennedy rarely swung left in establishment clause cases: he voted to ban prayers at public school graduations and sporting events because they "coerced" students into religious observation. Otherwise, he sided consistently against separation of church and state. Kennedy's successor, Justice Brett Kavanaugh, is even more conservative in this arena. While serving on the court of appeals, he authored an opinion in 2010's *Newdow v. Roberts* that ignored the *Lemon* test and championed a flimsier standard instead. In Kavanaugh's view, government-sponsored expression of religion is constitutional so long it does not "proselytize" or "disparage" a certain faith.

When *American Legion* hit the docket, then, the majority seemed poised to seal *Lemon*'s tomb for good. Alito and Kavanaugh had replaced the court's establishment clause swing votes. And Michael Carvin, the firebrand conservative litigator defending the monument, was gunning for *Lemon*. Carvin's brief attacked the test as "anti-historical," "oft-criticized," and ripe for repudiation. During oral arguments, Justice Neil Gorsuch twice dismissed the *Lemon* test as a "dog's breakfast" (translation: a complete mess). "Is it time," he pondered, "for this court to thank *Lemon* for its services and send it on its way?"

Not quite. In June, the Supreme Court handed down a decision upholding the Bladensburg cross *and* sparing *Lemon*. Justice Alito's majority opinion held that the *Lemon* test should not apply to "longstanding monuments, symbols, and practices" that are "religiously expressive."

Instead, these objects and practices should have a "presumption of constitutionality." It is difficult, Alito wrote, to divine the purpose of "monuments, symbols, or practices that were first established long ago." Moreover, their purpose as well as the message they convey may change over time. Here, for instance, the Bladensburg cross is "undoubtedly a Christian symbol," but it is also "a symbolic resting place," a "place for the community to gather" and honor veterans, and "a historical landmark." It has "acquired additional layers" of secular and "historical meaning" in the years since it was erected.

Alito also wrote that removing the Bladensburg cross and other long-standing religious monuments would "strike many as aggressively hostile to religion." There is thus a curious contradiction at the heart of his opinion: the cross is constitutional in part because it does not convey a purely Christian message, but *removing* it would convey an anti-Christian message.

Chief Justice John Roberts and Justices Stephen Breyer and Brett Kavanaugh all joined Alito's opinion in full. Justice Elena Kagan joined most of it but wrote a brief concurrence pushing back against a section highlighting the *Lemon* test's alleged "shortcomings." Breyer wrote a concurrence highlighting the fact that Alito's opinion applied only to older monuments, noting that contemporary efforts to build religious symbols could still be illegal. Oddly, Kavanaugh also wrote a concurrence claiming the opposite—that religious monuments are constitutional even if they are new. He then asserted that "this Court no longer applies the old test articulated in *Lemon*," which is no longer "good law." In other words, the court did not need to kill *Lemon* because it is already dead.

Gorsuch and Justice Clarence Thomas both wrote separately, concurring in the judgment only—meaning they agreed with Alito's bottom line but declined to join his opinion. Like Kavanaugh, Gorsuch bashed *Lemon* as a "misadventure" that the court had effectively "shelved." He also wrote that those disturbed by government displays of religion should not even have standing to sue, because "offense alone" does not inflict a constitutional injury. Thomas penned a more radical opinion, declaring that the establishment clause applies only to the federal government, not the states. (Under this theory, a state could establish an official religion without violating the U.S. Constitution.) He added that "because the *Lemon* test is not good law, we ought to say so."

Only Justice Ruth Bader Ginsburg, joined by Justice Sonia Sotomayor, dissented. Ginsburg, a strict church-state separationist, reminded her colleagues that the cross represents the "central theological claim of Christianity: that the son of God died on the cross, that he rose from the dead, and that his death and resurrection offer the possibility of eternal life." Using the cross "as a war memorial does not transform it into a secular symbol" and instead "elevates Christianity over other faiths, and religion over nonreligion." By maintaining the Bladensburg cross on public land, Maryland appears "to endorse its religious content," a plain violation of the establishment clause as interpreted by *Lemon* and its progeny.

Upon closer inspection, the vote in *American Legion* looks less like a 7–2 split and more like a 3–2–2–2 divide. Alito, Roberts, and Kavanaugh were happy to uphold the Bladensburg cross by trimming precedent; Thomas and Gorsuch craved a frontal assault on older decisions that cut against the cross. Breyer and Kagan sought out compromise, dwelling on the secular significance of the cross as a ninety-four-year-old war memorial. Ginsburg and Sotomayor, by contrast, demanded stringent separation of church and state to prevent the government from "suggesting official recognition" of one religion's "paramountcy."

The justices' fight over the *Lemon* test in *American Legion* may seem largely academic, a theoretical dispute bound to fascinate law professors and puzzle everyone else. But the fact that a seemingly straightforward decision devolved into so many separate opinions contesting the meaning and validity of *Lemon* should be a clue that there is something momentous afoot. And there is. The conservative justices are pummeling *Lemon* because they are laying the groundwork for a First Amendment revolution that would interpret the free exercise clause to *require* what *Lemon* forbids. Namely, the new majority wants to compel government subsidization of religion—and must hobble the establishment clause to succeed.

As constitutional guarantees go, the free exercise clause is remarkably unambiguous, as it bars the government from "prohibiting the free exercise" of religion. Everyone agrees that the framers of the Constitution saw this promise as vitally important to a free nation. In practice, though, it is not so simple to apply. For decades, the Supreme Court interpreted the clause to mandate state accommodations for religious belief. So, for instance, the court held in 1972's *Wisconsin v. Yoder* that states may not impose compulsory school attendance laws on the Amish because high school would interfere "with the religious development of the Amish child," infringing upon the community's "deep religious conviction."

Chapter 2

In 1990's *Employment Division v. Smith*, however, the Supreme Court upended this interpretation of free exercise. A Native American man, Alfred Smith, was fired from his job because he ingested peyote, a hallucinogen, for sacramental purposes. Oregon then denied Smith unemployment compensation because he was discharged for doing drugs. He requested an exemption, citing his First Amendment right to free exercise of religion. By a 5–4 vote, the Supreme Court reversed the many precedents, including *Yoder*, that compelled states to accommodate religious exercise. In his majority opinion, Scalia announced that moving forward, states could enforce any "neutral law of general applicability" against religious practitioners. Because Oregon's law fit the bill, Smith was out of luck.

Smith drew protests across the political and ideological spectrum. The decision even motivated a nearly unanimous Congress to pass the Religious Freedom Restoration Act in an effort to restore exemptions for believers. In 1993 the court somewhat tempered that criticism in *Church of Lukumi Babalu Aye v. City of Hialeah*, ruling that laws "targeting religious beliefs" to achieve "the suppression of religion" remained unconstitutional. Yet few laws actually "target" religion for disfavored treatment, so *Church of Lukumi* seemed like a rare exception to *Smith*'s rule.

Although it was authorized by Scalia, *Smith* is increasingly unpopular among jurists, scholars, and commentators on the Right. And in recent years, the Supreme Court's conservatives have begun chipping away at its foundations—using *Church of Lukumi* as their mallet. In a 2016 opinion Alito, joined by Roberts and Thomas, castigated his colleagues for refusing to hear a challenge to a Washington law obligating pharmacists to provide the emergency contraceptive Plan B. There was no evidence that the state had targeted Christians, only that it thought that all pharmacies should dispense emergency contraception even if individual pharmacists found this to be immoral. Yet that fact alone, Alito wrote, may suffice to prove unconstitutional "hostility toward religious objections."

"If this is a sign of how religious liberty claims will be treated in the years ahead," Alito warned, "those who value religious freedom have cause for great concern."

The next year, a majority of the court inched closer to Alito's views. In 2017's *Trinity Lutheran v. Comer*, the court heard an appeal from a Missouri church that claimed it had been subject to unlawful discrimination. The church, Trinity Lutheran, applied for a grant from the state to purchase a rubber playground surface for its preschool and day care facility. The State of Missouri turned down its application, citing a provision of the state constitution that prohibits the use of taxpayer money "directly or indirectly, in aid of any church, section or denomination of religion." The church filed suit, alleging a violation of its free exercise rights.

By a 7–2 vote, the Supreme Court agreed. Writing for the majority, Roberts wrote that Missouri had imposed "special disabilities" based on its "religious status." This "express discrimination against religious exercise," he wrote, violates the First Amendment, citing *Church of Lukumi*. "Trinity Lutheran was denied a grant simply because of what it is—a church," Roberts concluded. And the free exercise clause bars states from "singl[ing] out the religious for disfavored treatment."

All of the conservative justices as well as Kagan and Breyer agreed with Roberts. In a furious dissent Sotomayor, joined by Ginsburg, accused them of "a startling departure from our precedents." Not only is Missouri *permitted* to deny a grant to Trinity Lutheran, Sotomayor wrote, the state is *required* to deny the grant under the establishment clause. The church uses its playground to "assist the spiritual growth of the children," furthering its "religious mission." And for decades, the court had recognized that the establishment clause forbids "direct funding of religious activities." This cardinal rule predates the *Lemon* test but is enshrined in that standard's prohibition on government actions that "advance" religion. Now, suddenly, the court had turned the rule on its head, holding that states are not just allowed to fund religious activities but sometimes may also be compelled to do so.

Sotomayor read her lengthy *Trinity Lutheran* dissent from the bench, signaling her profound disagreement with the ruling. But the decision received little attention from the general public, perhaps because the stakes seemed relatively low and because two liberal justices supported the holding. In 2019, though, Kavanaugh upped the ante. When the court refused to hear a case called *Morris County v. Freedom from Religion Foundation*, Kavanaugh wrote an opinion laying out his interpretation of the free exercise clause. That opinion vindicated Sotomayor's worst fears about *Trinity Lutheran*.

Morris County involved twelve churches that sought to restore their facilities with historic preservation funds provided by the county. But like the Missouri Constitution, the New Jersey Constitution bars the use of taxpayer money to aid religion. Several churches sued, claiming a violation of their free exercise rights. A unanimous New Jersey Supreme Court ruled against them, pointing out that the funds would help the churches "conduct worship services and repair religious imagery." The court would not make taxpayers subsidize the literal exercise of religion.

Kavanaugh joined his colleagues' decision not to take the case due to "factual uncertainty about the scope of the [funding] program." But he made it clear that otherwise, he would have compelled New Jersey to provide historic preservation funds to houses of worship. The bar on funds for churches, he wrote, constitutes "pure discrimination against religion," a violation of the First Amendment's "bedrock principle of religious equality." Citing *Trinity Lutheran* and *Church of Lukumi*, Kavanaugh suggested that states cannot deny historic preservation funds "to religious organizations simply because the organizations are religious."

That is an extraordinary statement. For decades, the Supreme Court has read the establishment clause to limit the distribution of public funds to religious institutions, mandating that any taxpayer money be devoted to secular activities. Indeed, the *Lemon* test was originally devised to block state funding for parochial schools. Now, according to his *Morris County* opinion, Kavanaugh wants to use the free exercise clause to mandate the distribution of public funds to religious institutions—even if that money will aid religious activities. Alito and Gorsuch joined his opinion. And given the track records of Roberts and Thomas, there is little reason to doubt that five justices will seize the next opportunity to embark upon this First Amendment revolution.

It may arrive as soon as O.T. 2019. In June 2019, the court agreed to hear *Espinoza v. Montana Department of Revenue*. The case began as a challenge to a Montana law that uses tax credits to provide scholarships to children who attend private schools, including parochial institutions. Like Missouri and New Jersey, Montana's constitution bars the use of taxpayer money "in aid of any church" as well as religious schools. So, the Montana Supreme Court struck down the scholarship scheme, ruling that it ran afoul of this ban on public financing of religion.

The U.S. Supreme Court will decide whether this outcome violates religious schools' free exercise rights. In light of *Trinity Lutheran*, the court will probably say yes. Such a decision would affect every state that offers either school vouchers or Montana-style "tax credit scholarships" to children—nearly thirty in all. These states would have to let children use their vouchers or scholarships to attend religious schools. The court's decision could usher in a flood of public money to sectarian institutions that will help to fund the exercise of religion.

Under the *Lemon* test, state aid for religious activity would be an unconstitutional advancement of religion. But after *American Legion*, the conservative justices may be done with *Lemon*—and, more broadly, an establishment clause with any teeth. They have moved onto bigger things: turning *Church of Lukumi* into an exception that ate *Smith*'s rule. The main question now is whether Breyer and Kagan, the court's church-state moderates, will come along for the ride. This seems unlikely. Both wrote dissents to 2015's *Greece v. Galloway*, a 5–4 decision allowing town boards to open meetings with almost exclusively Christian prayers. Breyer and Kagan envision a First Amendment that allows for reasonable religious accommodations, not one that undermines states' ability to remain secular.

In the future, *American Legion* may be best remembered for the justices' shadowboxing over *Lemon*. *American Legion* might also be the last narrow religion decision handed down by the Roberts Court. Like *Lemon* before it, *Smith* could soon be "shelved," then killed off altogether. A jurisprudence of moderation, rooted in respect for government neutrality in a pluralist society, would be transformed into a rule that forces states—and, by extension, taxpayers—to help finance religious exercise. As Sotomayor noted in her *Trinity Lutheran* dissent, separation of church and state is not just some "constitutional slogan"; it is a "core protection for religious freedom." The conservative justices may praise religious liberty, most frequently in cases involving Christianity. But they seem uninterested in safeguarding the liberty of Americans who do not wish to fund faiths that flout their own beliefs.

Abortion Access Denied

When Justice Anthony Kennedy announced his retirement on June 27, 2018, he set off a wave of panic in the abortion rights movement. Kennedy long served as a swing vote on abortion. In 1992 he affirmed the central holding of *Roe v. Wade*, prohibiting laws that impose an "undue burden" on a woman's ability to terminate her pregnancy before viability, and in 2016 he cast the fifth vote invalidating a Texas law that foisted stringent regulations on abortion clinics. Kennedy appeared to be the one justice standing between *Roe* and oblivion—a fact that Donald Trump used to his advantage on the campaign trail when he promised to appoint justices who would overturn *Roe*. By stepping down, Kennedy gave Trump the chance to carry out his campaign pledge and consign *Roe* to the dustbin of history.

The president did not disappoint his supporters. To replace Kennedy, Trump selected Brett Kavanaugh, a court of appeals judge with a record of ruling against reproductive rights. Democratic senators grilled Kavanaugh about abortion during his nomination hearings, but the judge deftly avoided saying much of substance. He described *Roe* as "settled precedent" entitled to "respect," a vague answer likely directed at Senator Susan Collins of Maine. A Republican who claims to favor abortion rights, Collins held Kavanaugh's fate in her hands after nearly every Senate Democrat—and one Republican, Alaska's Lisa Murkowski—came out against his confirmation.

At the last minute, Collins endorsed Kavanaugh in a dramatic forty-three-minute floor speech. She insisted that he would not overturn *Roe* because he felt that precedent was "not something to be trimmed, narrowed, discarded, or overlooked." Collins also dismissed Christine Blasey Ford's allegations of sexual assault against Kavanaugh, speculating that she had confused him for someone else. The Senate then confirmed Kavanaugh by a vote of 50–48, the smallest margin in 137 years. As he was sworn in at the U.S. Supreme Court, protesters crossed a police line to rush the front steps and climb the two enormous statues that flank the front of the building. One depicts a woman wielding the scales of justice; the other depicts a man holding a sword.

It did not take long for an abortion case to land at the court. Just before Kavanaugh's confirmation, an appeals court refused to block a Louisiana abortion law virtually identical to the Texas statute struck down in 2016. The law would shutter all but one of Louisiana's abortion clinics and leave just one doctor in the entire state who could legally perform the procedure. Louisiana's law was set to take effect on February 8, 2019. If the Supreme Court's conservatives declined to halt it, their decision could signal an assault on the constitutional right to abortion access. And so, on the night of February 7, advocates on both sides awaited the court's decree, anxious to learn whether *Roe* and its progeny remain the law of the land.

No issue divides the Supreme Court—and perhaps the nation—like abortion. Although opinion polls indicate that a stable majority of Americans support *Roe*, a substantial minority of the country sees the ruling as wrong, dangerous, and even illegitimate. *Roe* has become a bugbear of the Republican Party and the conservative legal establishment, which cites the case as a leading example of gross judicial overreach. To *Roe*'s foes, the decision warped the U.S. Constitution to snatch a matter of profound public importance from the democratic process where it belongs. To its supporters, *Roe* enshrined a fundamental right of bodily autonomy into the constitution, ensuring that women's equal dignity does not depend on the outcome of elections.

When it was handed down in 1973, *Roe* was a bolt from the blue. At the time there was a burgeoning movement to liberalize abortion laws, but the procedure remained criminalized in most of the country. By a 7–2 vote the court swept away this legal regime, declaring that the Constitution safeguards a woman's right to abortion during the first three months of pregnancy (the first trimester). In the second trimester states could impose regulations to promote "the health of the mother," but only in the third trimester could they outlaw abortion, with exceptions for maternal health.

Roe helped fuel the rise of the religious Right as a dominating force in American politics. Ronald Reagan seized on opposition to the decision in order to help him win the presidency in 1980, and his Justice Department took the unusual step of asking the Supreme Court to overturn *Roe*.

The justices declined but scaled it back in the process, giving states more leeway to regulate abortion. By the time the court heard 1992's *Planned Parenthood v. Casey*, it appeared that a majority of the justices were prepared to overturn *Roe*. The case involved a challenge to a Pennsylvania law that, among other things, compelled women to wait twenty-four hours between consultation and abortion, hear about the risks of abortion as well as the age of the fetus, and notify spouses about their decision to terminate.

After the court heard arguments in *Casey*, five justices, including Kennedy, voted to uphold the entire Pennsylvania law and overturn *Roe*. Then Kennedy switched his vote. Rather than reverse *Roe*, he joined with Justices Sandra Day O'Connor and David Souter to uphold and modify it. Their plurality's opinion replaced *Roe*'s "rigid trimester framework" with the "undue burden" standard.

Under this test, the government "may enact regulations to further the health or safety of a woman seeking an abortion" but may not create "unnecessary health regulations" that impose a "substantial obstacle in the path of a woman seeking an abortion of a nonviable fetus." (Viability occurs around twenty-four weeks.) Using this standard, the plurality upheld every provision of the Pennsylvania law except one, the spousal notification requirement, as it "enables the husband to wield an effective veto over his wife's decision."

The *Casey* plurality had a lofty goal: to call "contending sides of a national controversy to end their national division by accepting a common mandate rooted in the Constitution." In that respect, it failed miserably. Abortion did not fade away as a controversy in American politics. The court too splintered over the true meaning of the test it had fashioned, and Kennedy drifted rightward on abortion. (Meanwhile, O'Connor was replaced by Justice Samuel Alito, who as a federal court of appeals judge had voted to uphold the very same spousal notification law that *Casey* struck down.) In 2007's *Gonzales v. Carhart*, Kennedy wrote a 5–4 decision upholding a federal law banning the safest procedure for second-trimester abortions. His opinion expressed disgust with the procedure while watering down the undue burden standard. This left many observers to speculate that the justice was prepared to overturn *Roe* and *Casey*.

Abortion rights activists put Kennedy to the test in 2016's *Whole Woman's Health v. Hellerstedt*, a challenge to Texas's targeted restrictions on abortion providers (or TRAP law). The Texas statute required abortion clinics to retrofit themselves as ambulatory surgical centers, a costly process that few could afford. The statute also directed abortion providers to obtain admitting privileges at a hospital within thirty miles of their clinic. Together, these regulations threatened to shutter all but ten clinics within the vast state's borders, forcing many women to drive hundreds of miles to terminate their pregnancies.

By a 5–3 vote the Supreme Court struck down both provisions, with Kennedy joining the liberals. (Justice Antonin Scalia had died several months earlier.) The court strengthened the undue burden standard, holding that it required courts to weigh the benefits of an abortion restriction against the burdens. The court then found that the Texas law provided no medical benefits to women— though it would shut down multiple clinics, compelling women to travel much farther to obtain an abortion. Because the statute imposed these hefty burdens without providing any actual benefits, the court concluded that Texas's law constituted an undue burden.

In theory, *Whole Woman's Health* should have ended a long stretch of uncertainty over abortion rights. The Supreme Court finally held that states cannot saddle abortion clinics with exorbitant regulations in the name of women's health unless they demonstrate that the regulations would help women. TRAP laws appeared to be doomed. Then Kennedy retired.

The Supreme Court is allowed to revisit its precedent; lower courts are not. So, it was a shock when in September 2018 the U.S. Court of Appeals for the Fifth Circuit upheld a Louisiana TRAP law identical to a provision of the Texas statute struck down in *Whole Woman's Health*. The Louisiana regulation required abortion providers to obtain admitting privileges at a hospital within thirty miles of their clinic—just as Texas had done earlier. The regulation would leave one doctor in one clinic in the entire state who could perform abortions. Under *Whole Woman's Health*, this outcome plainly imposes an undue burden on women.

Nevertheless, in *June Medical Services*, the Fifth Circuit upheld the Louisiana law. Judge Jerry Smith, a staunch conservative, first found that admitting privileges provide benefits to women by performing a "credentialing function." He then wrote that Louisiana doctors "sat on their hands" instead of trying to get these privileges. If these doctors tried harder, he asserted, most (but not all) could obtain them. Those who *did* get privileges could perform hundreds of extra abortions each year to pick up the slack from those who did not. Women might have to wait longer to obtain the procedure due to doctors' heightened workload but not long enough to suffer an undue burden.

Smith's accusation against the doctors in *June Medical Services* is refuted by the record. As Judge Patrick Higginbotham painstakingly demonstrated in his dissent, Louisiana's abortion providers did try to get admitting privileges but were refused—often *because* they performed abortions. In reality, no amount of "good-faith efforts" could have helped these doctors secure the necessary privileges. Only one abortion provider in the entire state had these privileges because he secured them before the new law took effect. And he testified that he would stop performing abortions if he became the last doctor in the state able to do so because he feared "violence and harassment."

More importantly, Higginbotham wrote, the very premise of Smith's opinion is flawed. Higginbotham stated that the admitting privileges requirement provides a "real" benefit to women, yet the Supreme Court held the precise opposite in *Whole Woman's Health*. There, the majority held that this requirement did not advance women's health in any way. Under the balancing test in *Whole Woman's Health*, Higginbotham explained, Smith was obligated to rule that the Louisiana law is unconstitutional, as it imposed real burdens without providing any benefits.

Smith, however, did not apply binding Supreme Court precedent, reading *Whole Woman's Health* to permit the exact kind of TRAP law that the ruling prohibits. Why? The likeliest explanation is that Smith believed that the Supreme Court would no longer apply its progressive precedent once Kennedy left the bench. Specifically, Smith may have hoped that Kavanaugh—then on the brink of confirmation—would reject his predecessor's abortion jurisprudence.

If so, Smith had good reason for optimism. Trump may have chosen Kavanaugh to fill Kennedy's seat precisely because of his antiabortion record on the federal bench. In 2017 as a judge on the U.S. Court of Appeals for the District of Columbia Circuit, Kavanaugh participated in *Garza v. Hargan.* The high-profile case involved Jane Doe, an undocumented minor who entered the United States illegally unaccompanied by her parents. The government placed Doe in a federally funded Texas shelter, where she discovered that she was pregnant and asked for an abortion.

Pursuant to Texas law, Doe obtained judicial bypass and underwent state-mandated counseling. But Trump administration officials then stepped in and forbade her from undergoing the procedure. They announced that they did not want to "facilitate" abortion by allowing Doe to obtain one while in federal custody. (Court filings later revealed that the administration applied this rule even though the minor was pregnant as a result of rape.)

With the help of the American Civil Liberties Union, Doe filed suit. The Department of Justice contended that she faced no undue burden; if Doe wanted an abortion, the government's lawyers argued, she should find a sponsor who would let her get one or self-deport. A federal judge disagreed, noting that the "burden" here was, in fact, absolute: for all practical purposes, the Trump administration had imposed a flat ban on Doe's ability to terminate. She had already tried to find a sponsor with no success, and she could not self-deport because abortion was illegal in her home country. The judge ordered the government to step aside and let Doe undergo the procedure.

Two days later, a three-judge panel from the D.C. Circuit (which included Kavanaugh) reversed that decision.

Kavanaugh issued an order granting the government more time to find a sponsor for Doe—even though she was already fifteen weeks pregnant. Texas bans abortion after twenty weeks, locating a sponsor can take months, and every additional week of pregnancy at that stage makes the procedure more dangerous. In a furious dissent, Judge Patricia Millett accused Kavanaugh of distorting "settled, binding Supreme Court precedent" to permit the administration's "astonishing power grab." The government, she wrote, cannot run down the clock by searching for a sponsor who *might* let her get an abortion; the government had to let her terminate immediately.

Millett's dissent soon became law. Four days after Kavanaugh's order the D.C. Circuit, sitting en banc (i.e., with every judge participating), reversed Kavanaugh's order and adopted Millett's position. Doe obtained her abortion shortly thereafter. It was Kavanaugh's turn to write a blistering dissent, and he filled his opinion with distinctive antiabortion rhetoric. He accused the majority of creating "a new right for unlawful immigrant minors" to "obtain immediate abortion on demand." Its decision, Kavanaugh wrote, was "inconsistent" with Supreme Court precedents upholding laws that force minors to procure parental consent or judicial bypass before undergoing an abortion.

Kavanaugh was not on the lengthy list of potential Supreme Court nominees that Trump issued during the campaign. A few weeks after the judge's *Garza* dissent, though, Trump revised his shortlist to include Kavanaugh. Less than a year later, he was sitting on the Supreme Court.

Did Kavanaugh's dissent catch Trump's eye? If so, it is easy to see why. In addition to its disparaging references to "abortion on demand," the opinion deftly repurposed precedent to cut back on the right to choose. As Millett noted, the Supreme Court has indeed upheld parental consent laws that delay minors' abortions by compelling them to get permission from their parents or a judge. But Doe had already complied with Texas's parental consent law and secured judicial bypass. The Trump administration sought to add an *additional* burden—as Millett put it, a "flat and categorical prohibition" on abortion. Contrary to Kavanaugh's claim, no Supreme Court precedent allows the government to impose a second burden beyond parental consent, let alone an obstacle that cannot be realistically surmounted.

When *June Medical Services* arrived at the Supreme Court, Kavanaugh's *Garza* dissent loomed large. Abortion providers asked the justices to stay the Fifth Circuit's decision in an emergency order, keeping the law on hold while they appealed. They faced steep odds. Kavanaugh seemed to be the swing vote if only by process of elimination: Justice Clarence Thomas has repeatedly stated his belief that abortion restrictions are constitutional. Chief Justice John Roberts had never voted to invalidate an antiabortion law, nor had Alito. All three justices dissented in *Whole Woman's Health*, indicating their belief that states could regulate abortion clinics out of existence. Justice Neil Gorsuch had channeled his predecessor, Scalia, on social issues, spurning progressive precedents rooted in constitutional "liberty." Would Kavanaugh lend the four liberal justices a fifth vote to *June Medical Services* to keep the Louisiana law on ice? Or would the five conservatives let the law take effect, essentially overturning *Whole Woman's Health* in an emergency order?

On the night of February 7, the Supreme Court issued its decree: a 5–4 order staying the Fifth Circuit's decision, thereby blocking the Louisiana law. But Kavanaugh hadn't swung left—instead, it was Roberts who joined the liberals to freeze the clinic regulation in a brief order. Thomas, Alito, and Gorsuch all dissented without opinion. Kavanaugh went the extra mile, writing a dissent effectively adopting Smith's position. The court, he wrote, should let Louisiana implement the law, with a "45-day transition period" during which abortion providers could try, once again, to gain admitting privileges. If they failed, they could return to district court and file another lawsuit, beginning the process anew. In the meantime, the women of Louisiana would be left with a single functioning abortion clinic at most.

Kavanaugh's dissent in *June Medical Services* bore a striking similarity to his position in *Garza*. In both cases, Kavanaugh professed respect for precedent while reshaping that precedent to reach an antiabortion outcome. (After all, his dissent implicitly accepted the notion that the admitting privileges create real benefits for women, which *Whole Woman's Health* rejected.) His approach lights the path forward for conservative legal advocates who fear that the court is unlikely to reverse *Roe* in one fell swoop. Instead of challenging *Roe* head-on, states can pass oblique attacks on abortion access; in upholding these laws, the Supreme Court's conservatives can chip away at *Roe* case by case. Eventually, the court will have destroyed the foundations of the constitutional right to choose. At that point, the court can overturn *Roe* or simply leave it on the books as a toothless precedent.

The Supreme Court's order in *June Medical Services* could have been the first step in that process. It was not, because Roberts sided with the liberals—the first time in his career on the bench that the chief justice has voted to block an abortion law. Although his vote came as a surprise, it is not difficult to understand. Roberts dissented in *Whole Woman's Health*, but he is an institutionalist who cares deeply about his court's prestige and legitimacy. He seems to have recognized that the Supreme Court does not typically overturn its precedents in an emergency order. Roberts's vote may also have been intended to remind lower court judges such as Smith not to disregard liberal precedent merely because Kavanaugh has replaced Kennedy. Finally, the chief justice probably sought to avoid the political firestorm that would result from an order allowing the Louisiana law to take effect.

Roberts could still dash the hopes of abortion rights advocates. Now that they have received their emergency stay, Louisiana's abortion providers must formally appeal the Fifth Circuit's decision to the Supreme Court so the justices can decide the case on the merits. With the Louisiana law squarely before him, Roberts may well prune *Whole Woman's Health* or overturn it altogether. The chief justice was not willing to let the Fifth Circuit reverse *Whole Woman's Health* on its own. But he might take aim at the precedent once it has been properly placed on the chopping block.

The Supreme Court dodged four other abortion controversies over the last term, declining to hear cases involving public funding for Planned Parenthood, "eugenics abortion," and a ban on second-trimester terminations and issuing a compromise decision in a dispute over state regulation of "fetal remains." Taken together, these four cases suggest that a majority of the justices are eager to avoid wading into the abortion quagmire whenever possible, though several conservative justices are losing patience with their colleagues' compromises.

In December 2018 the court refused to hear to hear *Gee v. Planned Parenthood of Gulf Coast* that centered on Planned Parenthood, an organization that provides abortions, contraception, reproductive health care, and other medical treatments. The group receives more than $500 million in public funding each year, mostly in the form of Medicaid reimbursements. (Planned Parenthood cannot use this money to cover abortion except in cases of rape, incest, or life endangerment.) In 2015, antiabortion activists released videos purporting to show Planned Parenthood employees selling fetal tissue, a violation of federal law. Several state investigations found no wrongdoing, but a slew of states moved to "defund" Planned Parenthood anyway by revoking its ability to receive Medicaid reimbursements.

Multiple patients sued, citing a federal law that requires states to provide these reimbursements to "qualified" providers. The federal courts of appeal divided on a threshold question: whether patients have a "private right of action" to challenge a state's determination that a provider is not "qualified." Five circuits found that patients did have such a right; one held that they did not. The Supreme Court routinely steps in to settle this kind of "circuit split," since federal law should be uniform throughout the country.

By a 6–3 vote, however, the Supreme Court declined to do so here. By tradition, four justices must agree to hear a case for the court to take it. (Taking a case is called granting certiorari, or "cert" for short.) When the court refuses to grant cert, it typically does not explain why. In accordance with that custom, the majority did not provide its reasons for denying cert in *Gee* despite the circuit split.

Occasionally when justices think that their colleagues should have granted cert in a particular case, they write dissents from denial of cert (referred to in shorthand as "dissents"). Thomas wrote one such dissent in *Gee*. Joined by Alito and Gorsuch, Thomas chided his colleagues for ducking the case. What, Thomas asked, "explains the Court's refusal to do its job here? I suspect it has something to do with the fact that some respondents in these cases are named 'Planned Parenthood.'" He added, "Some tenuous connection to a politically fraught issue does not justify abdicating our judicial duty. If anything, neutrally applying the law is all the more important when political issues are in the background."

The next abortion case, *Box v. Planned Parenthood of Indiana and Kentucky*, arrived in May. For months, the justices took no action on a challenge to an Indiana abortion law signed by Governor Mike Pence. The law imposed two new restrictions on abortion providers. First, clinics were obligated to bury or cremate fetal remains that resulted from an abortion unless patients chose to take them home; miscarriages were exempt. Second, physicians could not terminate a pregnancy on the basis of a fetus's race, sex, or disability, a provision meant to ban what the state called "eugenics abortions."

The U.S. Court of Appeals for the Seventh Circuit struck down both laws, finding that the ban on "eugenics abortions" obviously constituted an undue burden since it prohibited women from terminating certain pregnancies altogether. But the Seventh Circuit did not apply the undue burden test to the fetal remains rule, because

Planned Parenthood had not asked it to. Instead, for reasons that are not clear, the group alleged that this provision flunked a more lenient test, rational-basis review. Under this standard, a law need only be rationally related to a legitimate government interest to pass legal scrutiny. The Seventh Circuit found that the fetal remains rule failed even rational-basis review, because the state's interest in "humane and dignified disposal" was not "legitimate."

In an unsigned opinion, the Supreme Court reversed the Seventh Circuit's invalidation of the fetal remains provision by a 7–2 vote. The opinion held that states have a "legitimate interest in proper disposal of fetal remains" and that Indiana's law was rationally related to that interest. The majority "expresse[d] no view" on the tougher question—whether the rule imposes an "undue burden" by raising costs that clinics pass on to patients with no medical benefit. (Justices Ruth Bader Ginsburg and Sonia Sotomayor stated that they would have declined to hear the case.)

After upholding Indiana's fetal remains law, the justices unanimously refused to review the state's "eugenics abortion" ban. As usual, it did not give a reason for denying cert. Thomas wrote separately, explaining that "further percolation may assist our review of this issue of first impression." He also professed his support for the ban. Abortion, he wrote, "is an act rife with the potential for eugenic manipulation," and states should be empowered to stop women from terminating a fetus due to "unwanted characteristics." (There is no evidence that women in Indiana or elsewhere are terminating pregnancies on the basis of race or sex, though some women do get abortions due to fetal abnormalities.)

Thomas then provided a history lesson about the putative link between abortion and eugenics. He pointed out that many early supporters of birth control championed eugenicists' "goal of reducing undesirable populations." Margaret Sanger, the founder of Planned Parenthood, "was particularly open about the fact that birth control could be used for eugenic purposes," and "the eugenic arguments that she made in support of birth control apply with even greater force to abortion." Thomas deduced that "the individualized nature of abortion gives it even more eugenic potential than birth control."

To support his theory Thomas cited the work of Adam Cohen, an expert on eugenics movements. Cohen promptly wrote an article in *The Atlantic* titled "Clarence Thomas Knows Nothing of My Work" rebutting him. Thomas, Cohen explained, had "used the history of eugenics misleadingly, and in ways that could dangerously distort the debate over abortion." Eugenicists, including Sanger, did not support abortion, only contraception. Yet Thomas conflated the two through "a kind of historical guilt-by-association." His opinion was "an example of a common form of argumentation: the false analogy to a universally acknowledged historical atrocity."

More importantly, Thomas's argument has a faulty premise. "Between eugenic sterilization and abortion," Cohen wrote, "lie two crucial differences: who is making the decision, and why they are making it. In eugenic sterilization, the state decides who may not reproduce, and acts with the goal of 'improving' the population. In abortion, a woman decides not to reproduce, for personal reasons related to a specific pregnancy." Cohen concluded that Thomas "is absolutely wrong that individual women making independent decisions about their pregnancies are the eugenicists of our time."

Thomas wasn't finished denouncing abortion. A day after the court issued its last decisions of the term, it refused to hear *Harris v. West Alabama Women's Center*, which involved Alabama's ban on "dismemberment abortion." A district court found that the law would in practice ban abortion after fifteen weeks and blocked it as an undue burden. The U.S. Court of Appeals for the Eleventh Circuit begrudgingly affirmed that decision. Judges Edward Earl Carnes and Joel Fredrick Dubina, both appointed by George H. W. Bush, proclaimed that they would overturn *Roe* if they could. But because "there is only one Supreme Court, and we are not it," Carnes wrote, the court applied precedent to strike down the Alabama law.

Thomas does sit on the Supreme Court, and he seized on *Harris* to call for *Roe's* reversal. "This case," he wrote, "serves as a stark reminder that our abortion jurisprudence has spiraled out of control." The Supreme Court's abortion decisions are not "supported by the text of the Constitution," and "we cannot continue blinking the reality of what this Court has wrought." While Thomas felt that the case did "not present the opportunity to address our demonstrably erroneous 'undue burden' standard," he urged his colleagues to overturn *Roe* as soon as possible.

Five justices on the Supreme Court today have evinced a desire to curtail or abolish the constitutional right to abortion access. But they disagree on timing and strategy. Thomas is obviously keen to seize on the earliest opportunity to overturn *Roe*. Alito and Gorsuch are at a minimum prepared to uphold abortion restrictions that come before their court. And despite Senator Collins's avowal that Kavanaugh does not see precedent as "something to be trimmed," the justice has proved adept at trimming progressive precedent to reach an antiabortion result.

Roberts may therefore hold the cards here. Among court watchers, the conventional wisdom is that the chief justice will erode *Roe* and its progeny by methodically granting states more and more leeway to regulate abortion. The right to abortion access would die by a thousand cuts (or fewer). But if that is the plan, conservative lawmakers are making it more difficult by passing near-total abortion bans and asking the Supreme Court to overturn *Roe* and *Casey* all at once. In 2019 so far, five states—Georgia, Kentucky, Louisiana, Mississippi, and Ohio—have banned abortion after six weeks. Missouri banned abortion after eight weeks, while Alabama outlawed it from the moment of conception. Some legislative supporters of these measures have stated that they intend to test the limits of a post-Kennedy court, anticipating that five justices will now vote to abolish abortion rights.

The liberal justices seem concerned that their colleagues are poised to do just that. Contradicting Senator Collins's claim that Kavanaugh did not think precedent should be "discarded," the justice has voted to overturn precedent repeatedly throughout his first term. Most notably, he joined the conservatives in two 5–4 decisions that reversed decades-old precedents for no reason other than the fact that five justices did not like them anymore. Neither ruling was a blockbuster. One ruling, in *Franchise Tax Board of California v. Hyatt*, bolstered state sovereign immunity; the other, *Knick v. Township of Scott*, involved government taking of private property. But both decisions alarmed the liberal justices because of what they might portend.

In his *Hyatt* dissent, Justice Stephen Breyer, joined by his three liberal colleagues, condemned the majority's approach to precedent as "dangerous." He also cited a section of *Casey* laying out the importance of precedent. "Today's decision," Breyer warned, "can only cause one to wonder which cases the Court will overrule next."

Supreme Court justices do not issue warnings much clearer than that.

The Libertarian Court?

Shifting Views on Criminal Justice

Every term, the U.S. Supreme Court hands down several 5–4 decisions that divide along predictable ideological lines. The five Republican nominees rule for a conservative outcome that seems to favor the Republican Party, while the Democratic nominees dissent on liberal grounds. For those who see the court as an independent branch—not some superlegislature practicing politics under the guise of law—these cases can be dispiriting. They make the justices look like "junior varsity politicians," to borrow Justice Elena Kagan's phrase, rather than apolitical jurists applying the law in a neutral fashion.

Criminal justice cases can provide a welcome relief from this phenomenon. When it comes to enforcing the U.S. Constitution's protections for criminal defendants, the court often splinters along unusual lines that do not track partisan ideology. The 2019 term's criminal cases were especially unpredictable, uniting peculiar bedfellows from opposite wings of the court. These cases also revealed sharp disagreements between President Donald Trump's nominees, Justices Neil Gorsuch and Brett Kavanaugh, on the rights of the accused. This chapter explores six rulings that scrambled the court's usual alliances as the justices fought over constitutional safeguards for criminal defendants.

Timbs v. Indiana

The first major criminal justice decision handed down in the 2019 term involved civil asset forfeiture, derided by its critics as policing for profit. This practice allows law enforcement to seize cash or property from individuals suspected of wrongdoing, even if they have not been convicted or even charged with a crime. The abuses of forfeiture are well documented. In one notorious incident, Philadelphia prosecutors seized a couple's house because their son was arrested with $40 worth of drugs. Journalists at the *Washington Post* and the *New Yorker* have published shocking reports on the rise of "highway interdiction," a technique through which police aggressively stop motorists, accuse them of a crime, and demand that they turn over anything of value—cash, jewelry, even their cars. The motorists are let go with a warning and a threat that if they seek restitution, they will be charged and imprisoned.

Tyson Timbs experienced this system firsthand. Unlike many victims of civil asset forfeiture, Timbs was convicted of a crime. In 2015, he was charged with selling four grams of heroin in Indiana and pleaded guilty. But he was not forced to forfeit his property as part of his criminal conviction. Instead, the state attempted to seize Timbs's Land Rover SUV, valued at $42,000. The maximum fine for his offense was $10,000. Because Timbs allegedly used his Land Rover to transport drugs, however, Indiana asserted a right to seize and sell it.

Timbs alleged a violation of his rights under the Eighth Amendment, which bars the imposition of "excessive fines." He quickly ran into a problem. The Supreme Court has recognized that when the government seizes an individual's property in connection with a crime, it has imposed a "fine" under the Eighth Amendment. The court has also held that such "fines" may not be "grossly disproportionate" to an offense but has never expressly held that this right applies against the states. Indiana cited this fact to defend the forfeiture of Timbs's SUV.

To understand this argument, it is important to remember that the Bill of Rights initially applied only to the federal government, not the states. The first ten amendments were designed to appease Anti-Federalists who feared that the new national government would become tyrannical. After the American Civil War, Congress recognized that states too could oppress civil liberties: southern states censored free speech, suppressed religious exercise, and ignored due process to maintain slavery. Congress intended that the Fourteenth Amendment "incorporate" the Bill of Rights against the states. In relevant part, the amendment declares that "no State shall make or enforce any law which shall abridge the privileges or immunities of citizens of the United States; nor shall any State deprive any person of life, liberty, or property, without due process of law."

Throughout the twentieth century, the Supreme Court applied various provisions of the Bill of Rights to the states. By 2018, virtually all of its guarantees applied equally against the federal and state governments. Notably, the court *had* incorporated the Eighth Amendment's more famous provision, a bar on "cruel and unusual punishments," but had not had an occasion to incorporate the ban on excessive fines. Timbs was asking the court to finish the job.

At oral arguments, the justices appeared eager to do just that. In a remarkable exchange with Indiana solicitor general Thomas Fisher, Justice Neil Gorsuch sounded incredulous that the state opposed the incorporation of the excessive fines clause.

"Can we just get one thing off the table?" Gorsuch asked. "We all agree that the excessive fines clause is incorporated against the states. . . . Can we at least agree on that?" When Fisher hedged, the justice noted that most of the Bill of Rights was incorporated "in, like, the 1940s."

"And here we are in 2018, still litigating incorporation of the Bill of Rights," Gorsuch said. "Really? Come on, General."

It came as no surprise, then, when the justices unanimously incorporated the clause in February 2019. Justice Ruth Bader Ginsburg's opinion for the court traced the right against excessive fines back to the Magna Carta through the English Bill of Rights and the Virginia Declaration of Rights, all of which influenced the U.S. Constitution. When the Fourteenth Amendment was ratified, thirty-five of the thirty-seven states explicitly barred excessive fines. And during the debate over ratification, congressmen hoped that their amendment would stop southern states from using punitive fines to "subjugate newly freed slaves."

The Fourteenth Amendment's due process clause, Ginsburg noted, "incorporates the protections contained in the Bill of Rights" if they are "fundamental to our scheme of ordered liberty" or "deeply rooted in this Nation's history and tradition." History demonstrates that the guarantee against excessive fines fits both categories and therefore applies against the states.

While the court was unanimous on the bottom line, Justice Clarence Thomas wrote separately to quibble with Ginsburg's reasoning. Thomas rejected the notion that the due process clause protects "substantive rights" that have "nothing to do with 'process.'" The clause bars the government from depriving individuals of "life, liberty, or property" *without due process of law*, which Thomas views as an exclusively procedural protection. To incorporate the Bill of Rights, the court has held that certain aspects of "liberty" are so fundamental that no amount of due process can justify their revocation. According to Thomas, that approach validates a "legal fiction." He would apply the excessive fines clause through the privileges or immunities clause, which protects "privilege[s] of American citizenship."

Thomas's quarrel with the majority is not just academic. His distaste for "substantive due process" is a reaction to the Supreme Court's habit of locating new rights in the "liberty" of the due process clause. Specifically, the court has found that the rights to abortion access (1973's *Roe v. Wade*) and of same-sex couples to marry (2015's *Obergefell v. Hodges*) derive from this constitutional "liberty." In his *Timbs* concurrence, Thomas took a swipe at these decisions; he dismissed *Roe* as "notoriously incorrect" and mocked *Obergefell*'s logic as "border[ing] on meaningless." The justice could not join an opinion that rested on a doctrine he despises, even though he believed that Ginsburg reached the right outcome.

Gorsuch also wrote a brief concurrence backing Thomas. "As an original matter," Gorsuch wrote, "I acknowledge, the appropriate vehicle for incorporation may well be the Fourteenth Amendment's Privileges or Immunities Clause, rather than, as this Court has long assumed, the Due Process Clause." But because "nothing in this case turns on that question," he signed onto Ginsburg's opinion. It seems that Gorsuch is willing to part ways with his predecessor on this matter: Justice Antonin Scalia scorned the privileges or immunities theory as "the darling of the professoriate"; when a lawyer brought it up during arguments, Scalia asked if he was "bucking for a place on some law school faculty."

The decision in *Timbs* will not automatically curb civil asset forfeiture. Ginsburg did not announce whether Indiana's seizure of the Land Rover was "grossly disproportionate," sending that question back down to the lower court instead. Yet the Supreme Court has left the "grossly disproportionate" standard hazy, and judges have struggled to determine when, exactly, forfeiture crosses the constitutional line. *Timbs* won't help them. In the near future, the Supreme Court will likely take another excessive fines case to clarify the contours of the Eighth Amendment. Until then, *Timbs* may have created a constitutional right that no court knows how to enforce.

Garza v. Idaho

The Sixth Amendment states that in "all criminal prosecutions, the accused shall . . . have the Assistance of Counsel for his defence." For decades, the Supreme Court has interpreted that guarantee to ensure *effective* assistance of counsel. In 2000's *Roe v. Flores-Ortega*, the court held that a defense attorney's performance is constitutionally deficient when it "deprives a defendant of an appeal that he otherwise would have taken." In other words, when a defendant asks his lawyer to appeal a verdict and his lawyer refuses, the defendant has suffered a Sixth Amendment violation and is entitled to a new appeal.

That is exactly what happened in *Garza*. The defendant, Gilberto Garza Jr., begged his attorney to appeal, but no appeal was filed before the legal deadline. Garza alleged a violation of his rights under *Flores-Ortega*, but there was a catch: he had pleaded guilty and, in the process, signed an appeal waiver. In light of that waiver, the Idaho Supreme Court held that Garza was not entitled to a new appeal, reasoning that he had forfeited his right to any "appellate proceeding."

By a 6–3 vote, the U.S. Supreme Court reversed that decision. Justice Sonia Sotomayor wrote the majority opinion, joined by the liberals, Chief Justice John Roberts, and Justice Brett Kavanaugh. Sotomayor pointed out that defendants who sign an appeal waiver do not give up all their claims. Every jurisdiction treats "at least some claims as unwaiveable," she wrote, including "the right to challenge whether the waiver itself is valid and enforceable—for example, on the grounds that it was unknowing or involuntary." Thus, "a defendant who has signed an appeal waiver does not, in directing counsel to file a notice of appeal, necessarily undertake a quixotic or frivolous quest." Lawyers have a constitutional duty to follow their clients' instructions even if an appeal seems tough to win.

In dissent, Justice Thomas wrote that refusing to appeal "was the only professionally reasonable course of action for counsel under the circumstances." An appeal, he noted, "places the defendant's plea agreement in jeopardy" and could result in a harsher sentence for Garza. Justices Samuel Alito joined this part of his dissent, as did Gorsuch. But then in a section joined only by Gorsuch, Thomas took aim at the cornerstone of modern Sixth Amendment law: 1963's *Gideon v. Wainwright*, which compelled states to provide a court-appointed attorney to indigent defendants.

Gideon, Thomas asserted, has no basis in "the original meaning" of the Constitution. Accordingly, the court should "hesitate before further extending our precedents and imposing additional costs on the taxpayers and the Judiciary. History proves that the States and the Federal Government are capable of making the policy determinations necessary to assign public resources for appointed counsel."

Many public defenders would disagree with that statement. Lorelei Laird's 2017 article "Starved of Money for Too Long, Public Defender Offices Are Suing—And Starting to Win" in the *American Bar Association Journal* found that public defenders around the country are underpaid and overworked. Many public defenders must handle hundreds of cases a year—far too many for any one lawyer to represent. As a result, clients languish behind bars for weeks, even months, before consulting with their counsel. Some civil rights groups have filed lawsuits against states that slashed their public defender budget so dramatically that thousands of defendants are left without representation. Around 80 percent of Americans charged with a crime rely on public defenders for representation, yet the vast majority of states as well as the federal government are starving public defenders of funding.

Garza foreshadowed stark disagreements between Gorsuch and Kavanaugh on criminal justice. While Gorsuch signed onto Thomas's repudiation of *Gideon*, Kavanaugh joined Sotomayor's majority opinion in full. The chasm between the two justices would grow wider over the next four months.

Gamble v. United States

The Fifth Amendment states that no person may be "twice put in jeopardy of life or limb" for "the same offence." That guarantee provides a constitutional shield against "double jeopardy," successive prosecutions against an individual for the same crime. The Fifth Amendment ensures that if you are put on trial and acquitted, prosecutors cannot try you a second time hoping for better luck. And if you are convicted, prosecutors cannot wait by the prison gates, pick you up upon your release, and try you again for the same crime.

But for 170 years, the Supreme Court has found an exception to this rule, and it's a big one. Under the separate sovereigns doctrine, the federal government and state governments can try you separately for the same alleged misdeed. That is what happened to Terance Gamble after Alabama authorities caught him carrying a firearm illegally. Alabama prosecutors first brought charges under state law and secured a 1-year prison sentence. Then federal prosecutors, dissatisfied with that sentence, brought charges under *federal* law, adding nearly 3 years to Gamble's sentence. He then asked the Supreme Court to overturn the separate sovereigns doctrine and hold that two prosecutions for the same crime violate the Constitution, no matter who is doing the prosecuting.

By coincidence, *Gamble* arrived at the Supreme Court just as Special Counsel Robert Mueller secured convictions against a number of Trump's associates, including his former campaign chairman Paul Manafort. Trump vigorously criticized Mueller's prosecution of Manafort and praised his friend as a "brave man." If the president pardoned Manafort for his federal crimes, state prosecutors could still bring charges thanks to the separate sovereigns doctrine. If the Supreme Court overturned that doctrine, state prosecutors might be constitutionally forbidden from charging Manafort—meaning a presidential pardon would keep him out of prison for good.

At oral arguments, it became clear that the separate sovereigns doctrine was here to stay. Only Ginsburg and Gorsuch were skeptical of the rule; the remaining justices seemed to think that at a minimum, the court should respect a doctrine with roots in the 1850s. In June, the court issued a predictable 7–2 ruling upholding the separate sovereigns rule. A crime "under one sovereign's laws," Alito wrote for the majority, "is not 'the same offence' as a crime under the laws of another sovereign." And because no "historical evidence" proves otherwise, Alito saw "no reason to abandon" this long-standing interpretation of the clause.

Ginsburg and Gorsuch wrote separate dissents that made the same basic point. "The notion that the Federal Government and the States are separate sovereigns," Ginsburg wrote, overlooks the fact that "'ultimate sovereignty' resides in the *governed*." If a crime offends a "sovereign," that sovereign "is the people," the "original fountain of all legitimate authority." Similarly, Gorsuch wrote that "the federal and state governments are but two expressions of a single and sovereign people."

This libertarian vision of sovereignty failed to win over a majority of the court, which saw no compelling reason to overturn a well-established precedent. Thomas wrote a concurrence reiterating that he does not believe in respecting precedent when it is "demonstrably erroneous." Adhering to an incorrect decision, he declared, "disregards the supremacy of the Constitution and perpetuates a usurpation of the legislative power." It does not matter if hundreds of lower courts have applied a precedent throughout the country over the course of decades or centuries. "When faced with a demonstrably erroneous precedent," Thomas concluded, "my rule is simple: We should not follow it." (It was a bit odd that Thomas chose to write this attack on precedent as he voted to uphold precedent.)

The criminal defense bar was hoping that *Gamble* would create a Fifth Amendment revolution. Prosecutors worried that the case would hinder their ability to keep dangerous criminals off the streets, while Trump's critics feared that it might amplify the power of presidential pardons. In the end, *Gamble* made no change to the law at all. Stability still has some purchase at this Supreme Court.

Flowers v. United States

The facts of *Flowers* read like a nightmare straight out of the Jim Crow South. A white Mississippi prosecutor, Doug Evans, prosecuted a black man, Curtis Flowers, for the same crime six times in search of a capital conviction. At each trial, Evans used peremptory strikes—which allow trial attorneys to remove prospective jurors without providing a reason—on as many blacks as he could. In 1986's *Batson v. Kentucky*, the Supreme Court ruled that striking black jurors on account of their race violates the equal protection clause. Yet Evans appeared to believe that his courtroom was a *Batson*-free zone.

At Flowers's first trial Evans secured an all-white jury, which convicted Flowers for a gruesome 1996 murder and sentenced him to death. The Mississippi Supreme Court reversed the conviction due to prosecutorial misconduct. (Evans had baselessly disputed the credibility of a defense witness and mentioned facts not in evidence.) At Flowers's second trial, Evans again struck every black potential juror, but the judge found a *Batson* violation and seated one. The jury issued a guilty verdict that the Mississippi Supreme Court reversed again because Evans engaged in similar misconduct. At Flowers's third trial, Evans attempted to strike every potential black juror; the jury convicted, but the Mississippi Supreme Court reversed, describing Evans's efforts as the strongest "case of racial discrimination . . . we have ever seen in the context of a *Batson* challenge."

At Flowers's fourth and fifth trials, Evans was unable to strike every black prospective juror. Both resulted in a mistrial due to hung juries. At Flowers's sixth trial, Evans struck five of six black prospective jurors. Flowers was convicted and sentenced to death. By a 5–4 vote, the Mississippi Supreme Court upheld his conviction. Over the course of six trials, Evans had struck forty-one of forty-two black prospective jurors.

Oral arguments did not go well for Mississippi when *Flowers* landed at the U.S. Supreme Court. Kavanaugh seemed particularly appalled by the record before him. He grilled Mississippi special assistant attorney General Jason Davis after Davis asked the justices to "disengage this troubling history" and look only at Flowers's sixth trial.

"You said, 'if we take the history out of the case,'" Kavanaugh said. "We *can't* take the history out of the case." He added, "It was 42 potential African American Americans and 41 are stricken, right? . . . That's relevant, correct?" Later he asked Hunt, "And can you say, as you sit here today . . . you have confidence in . . . how this all transpired in this case?"

Hunt told the justice that he did "have confidence in this record." Kavanaugh wasn't convinced. Three months later, he authored a 7–2 decision throwing out Flowers's conviction. Kavanaugh's opinion painted a blunt picture of Evans's racism, though the justice attributed the prosecutor's actions to "the state":

> The state employed its peremptory strikes to remove as many black prospective jurors as possible. The State appeared to proceed as if *Batson* had never been decided. The State's relentless, determined effort to rid the jury of black individuals strongly suggests that the State wanted to try Flowers before a jury with as few black jurors as possible, and ideally before an all-white jury.

"We cannot ignore that history," Kavanaugh wrote, echoing his statement at oral arguments. "We cannot take that history out of the case."

Kavanaugh also highlighted "dramatically disparate questioning of black and white prospective jurors in the jury selection process for Flowers' sixth trial." Prosecutors "asked the five black prospective jurors who were struck a total of 145 questions." Meanwhile, they asked "the 11 seated white jurors a total of 12 questions." Each prospective black juror was asked an average of 29 questions; each seated white juror was asked an average of 1 question.

By "asking a lot of questions of the black prospective jurors," Kavanaugh wrote, "a prosecutor can try to find some pretextual reason—any reason—that the prosecutor can later articulate to justify what is in reality a racially motivated strike." And a court "confronting that kind of pattern cannot ignore it." This "lopsidedness" can indicate that the prosecutor was attempting to "disguise a discriminatory intent."

Assessing the evidence, Kavanaugh found that Evans had run afoul of *Batson*, striking at least one juror on account of her race. The equal protection clause, he wrote, does not permit a prosecutor to "strike a black juror based on an assumption or belief that the black juror would favor a black defendant." Because that is obviously what Evans did here, Flowers's conviction cannot stand. (Evans still serves as district attorney and could handle Flowers's seventh trial, though he has permanently tainted the case with racism.)

Kavanaugh's opinion in *Flowers* draws from *Foster v. Chatman*, a 7–1 decision issued in 2016. Writing the majority in *Foster*, Chief Justice Roberts laid out smoking-gun evidence discovered long after trial proving that the state had discriminated against black potential jurors. Prosecutors highlighted the names of black potential jurors in green, noting that green highlighting "represents Blacks." They identified black potential jurors as B#1, B#2, and B#3 and wrote "N" for "no" next to their names. They compared these potential jurors and wrote, "If it comes down to having to pick one of the black jurors, [this one] might be okay." Prosecutors secured an all-white jury, which convicted the black defendant and sentenced him to death. It was all too much for Roberts, who found a glaring *Batson* violation.

Only Thomas dissented in *Foster*, on the grounds that the court should not have let the defendant "relitigate his *Batson* claim by bringing this newly discovered evidence to the fore." Thomas has made no effort to conceal his distaste for *Batson* cases; during arguments in *Flowers*, he broke his customary silence to ask about "the race of the jurors" whom Flowers's lawyer had struck; the jurors were white. It was Thomas's first question in three years.

Thomas dissented again in *Flowers*, joined in part by Gorsuch. Thomas held nothing back, accusing the majority of taking Flowers's case because it wanted to "scorn" Mississippi state courts or perhaps "because the case has received a fair amount of media attention." The media, Thomas warned, often prefers "to titillate rather than to educate and inform." (He was probably referring to the popular podcast *In the Dark*, which put forth a staggering amount of evidence suggesting that Flowers is innocent.) Thomas scorned Kavanaugh's opinion as "manifestly incorrect," nothing more than an "entertaining melodrama." The court, Thomas insisted, should defer to the trial judge's decision to accept Evans's stated reasons for striking black prospective jurors.

But the most astonishing portion of Thomas's dissent—which Gorsuch did not join—called on the court to overturn *Batson* altogether. Prosecutors, Thomas wrote, should be allowed to make "generalizations" about jurors on the basis of race, because "race matters in the courtroom."

"The racial composition of a jury matters," Thomas explained, "because racial biases, sympathies, and prejudices still exist. This is not a matter of 'assumptions,' as *Batson* said. It is a matter of reality." Attorneys for both the state and the defendant should therefore be allowed to use peremptory strikes on jurors because of race. Doing so would restore "fairness of trials for the defendant whose liberty is at stake and to the People who seek justice under the law."

There was a fascinating dynamic at play in *Flowers* as the court's only black justice disparaged his colleagues' attempt to eradicate racism from the courtroom. Kavanaugh's majority opinion is a full-throated paean to racial tolerance; Thomas's dissent is a world-weary protest that it is impossible to ignore race in jury selection and is foolish to try. There is not much middle ground between Thomas and his colleagues here; not even Gorsuch joined his assault on *Batson*. When it comes to racist prosecutions, Thomas stands alone.

United States v. Davis

In two 5–4 decisions handed down toward the end of the term, Gorsuch joined the liberals to invalidate federal laws that offended his unique conception of crime and punishment. The first of these rulings, *Davis*, allowed him to channel his inner Scalia in a move that spurred Kavanaugh to accuse him of driving the court "off the constitutional cliff."

Davis completed a trilogy of decisions that has reinvigorated the court's void-for-vagueness jurisprudence. Under this doctrine, a criminal law infringes upon due process if it is so vague that it fails to give ordinary people fair notice of the conduct it proscribes or if it is so standardless that it engenders arbitrary enforcement. The first entry in the void-for-vagueness series, 2015's *Johnson v. United States*, involved a provision of the Armed Career Criminal Act (ACCA) that imposed a fifteen-year mandatory minimum sentence on a federal firearms offender with three prior convictions for a "violent felony." What qualifies as a "violent felony"? Among other things, "conduct that presents a serious potential risk of physical injury to another."

Here's the problem. ACCA requires courts to use a framework called "the categorical approach" to decide whether a felony "presents a serious potential risk of physical injury." As Scalia explained in his *Johnson* opinion, the categorical approach requires a court to ask "how the law defines the offense" and *not* "how an individual offender might have committed it on a particular occasion." To do so, a court must envision "the ordinary case" and ask "whether that abstraction presents a serious potential risk of physical injury."

ACCA demanded this bizarre approach because it attempted to squeeze fifty states' laws into a capacious federal standard. The statute was intended to shunt repeat state offenders into federal prison if their state offenses were "violent." But each state defines its laws differently, and it is isn't always clear when a state crime might involve violence. Earlier decisions illustrate this conundrum. The Supreme Court found that ACCA covers Indiana's ban on fleeing law enforcement in a vehicle, because "the determination to elude capture makes a lack of concern" for others' safety "an inherent part of the offense." On the other hand, the court held that ACCA does *not* cover New Mexico's ban on driving under the influence, because intoxicated driving does not inherently involve "purposeful, violent, and aggressive conduct." The ordinary person would struggle to understand how fleeing the police is somehow more intrinsically violent than drunk driving (which, according to the Centers for Disease Control and Prevention, kills twenty-nine Americans a day).

In *Johnson*, Scalia put a stop to this guessing game by striking down the residual clause. "Nine years' experience trying to derive meaning from the residual clause," he wrote, "convinces us that we have embarked upon a failed enterprise." The court could not forge a reliable test to determine when "the ordinary case" of a given crime presents "serious potential risk" of injury. "Invoking so shapeless a provision to condemn someone to prison for 15 years to life," Scalia concluded, "does not comport with the Constitution's guarantee of due process."

In 2018 the court issued *Sessions v. Dimaya*, the second entry in the void-for-vagueness trilogy. *Dimaya* involved a law that allowed the government to deport any alien convicted of an "aggravated felony." The law defined an aggravated felony as, among other things, an offense "that, by its nature, involves a substantial risk that physical force against the person or property of another may be used in the course of committing the offense." By a 5–4 vote, with Gorsuch joining the liberals, the court struck it down. The provision, Justice Elena Kagan wrote in her majority opinion, was "similarly worded" to ACCA's residual clause and contained the same vagueness that rendered that clause unlawful.

There was, however, a crucial distinction between the laws in *Johnson* and *Dimaya*. While the former imposed a prison sentence, the latter compelled only deportation. And the government argued that "a less searching form of the void-for-vagueness doctrine applies" in the immigration context. Kagan rejected that distinction, explaining that deportation is a "drastic measure" that may be "may be of greater concern to a convicted alien" than a jail sentence.

Gorsuch parted ways from the liberals on this point, contending that any deprivation of liberty or property is subject to scrutiny for vagueness. Why, he asked, "would due process require Congress to speak more clearly when it seeks to deport a lawfully resident alien than when it wishes to subject a citizen to indefinite civil commitment, strip him of a business license essential to his family's living, or confiscate his home?" He could "think of no good answer." Gorsuch also wrote that void-for-vagueness doctrine owes "equal debt" to due process and "separation of powers," the division of authority between the branches of government. The Constitution "does not license judges to craft new laws to govern future conduct" or let "police and prosecutors" shape "a vague statute's contours through their enforcement decisions."

After *Dimaya*, the outcome of *Davis*—the final entry in the void-for-vagueness trilogy—seemed preordained. The case involves a federal law that lengthens the prison sentence for certain firearms offenders who use a gun in a "crime of violence." The law defines a "crime of violence" almost exactly as the statute in *Dimaya* did: an offense that, "by its nature, involves a substantial risk that physical force against the person or property of another may be used in the course of committing the offense."

Writing for a 5–4 majority, Gorsuch struck down the law. He began his opinion, which was joined by the four liberals, with an ode the void-for-vagueness doctrine:

> In our constitutional order, a vague law is no law at all. Only the people's elected representatives in Congress have the power to write new federal criminal laws. And when Congress exercises that power, it has to write statutes that give ordinary people fair warning about what the law demands of them. Vague laws transgress both of those constitutional requirements. They hand off the legislature's responsibility for defining criminal behavior to unelected prosecutors and judges, and they leave people with no sure way to know what consequences will attach to their conduct. When Congress passes a vague law, the role of courts under our Constitution is not to fashion a new, clearer law to take its place, but to treat the law as a nullity and invite Congress to try again.

This passage perfectly captures Gorsuch's writing style—maddeningly grandiloquent to his detractors, vivid and forceful to his fans.

Relying on *Johnson* and *Dimaya*, Gorsuch made quick work of the statute, finding that it "provides no reliable way to determine which offenses qualify as crimes of violence and thus is unconstitutionally vague." In an uncharacteristically irate dissent, Kavanaugh—joined by Roberts, Thomas, and Alito—reproved the ruling as a "serious mistake" that would let "many dangerous offenders . . . walk out of prison early."

The quarrel between Gorsuch and Kavanaugh boils down to a philosophical dispute about the role of courts in American democracy. Kavanaugh wanted to rewrite the statute to make it less vague, justifying his efforts by citing the "severe" consequences of its invalidation. The majority, he warned, threatened to "undermine safety in American communities" by allowing violent offenders to leave prison early. To Gorsuch, these "social policy consequences" are irrelevant. A judge's job is to interpret the law as written, not modify its scope to comport with the Constitution. While "Congress always remains free to adopt" a less vague standard, the court cannot do Congress's job for it.

Gorsuch and Kavanaugh are alike in many ways. They attended the same high school, clerked for the same justice (Kennedy), and were appointed by the same president. But their views on government power sometimes diverge in momentous ways. Two days after Gorsuch handed down his decision in *Davis*, that divergence grew even more evident.

United States v. Haymond

The Sixth Amendment guarantees a trial by jury to "the accused" in "all criminal prosecutions." In 2000's *Apprendi v. New Jersey*, the Supreme Court ruled that this guarantee requires that the government prove to a jury, beyond a reasonable doubt, every element of a crime that raises the maximum sentence. In 2013's *Alleyne v. United States*, the court held that the government must also prove to a jury every element of a crime that raises the minimum sentence. Both decisions were decided by a 5–4 vote, dividing the court into formalists and pragmatists rather than liberals and conservatives, and were immensely controversial. Before *Apprendi* and *Alleyne*, countless laws gave judges discretion to heighten sentences on the basis of facts not proved to a jury. After these decisions, judges were obligated to let a jury find facts relevant to sentencing.

In *Haymond*, the court asked whether the rule laid down in these precedents applied to the federal "supervised release" system, which Congress created after it abolished parole in 1984. Under this system, convicted offenders are sentenced to a term of imprisonment and, after that, a period of supervised release. During this stretch of conditional freedom, offenders must abide by certain terms such as drug testing. If they violate the terms, they can be sent back to prison for the remainder of their supervised release.

At issue in *Haymond* is the law that altered this arrangement for offenders convicted of certain sex offenses, which sends these offenders back to prison for violating the terms of their release and is undoubtedly constitutional. But instead of sending them back to prison for their original conviction, the statute compels judges to impose *additional* prison time for the new offense. Judges may find these individuals guilty of a new offense under a "preponderance of the evidence" standard, not the "beyond a reasonable doubt" standard typically required by due process. And judges make this finding without a jury's involvement.

Andre Haymond's case illustrates this scheme in action. At age eighteen, Haymond was convicted of possessing several images of child pornography. A judge sentenced him to a thirty-eight-month prison term, followed by ten years of supervised release. After Haymond was released from prison, government agents accused him of possessing additional child pornography. He contested their claim in a proceeding that poked many holes in the government's case. The judge announced that "if this were a criminal trial and the Court were the jury, the United States would have lost." But under the lenient standard prescribed by the law, the judge found it "more likely than not" that Haymond had downloaded the images. Under the law at issue, this finding required the judge to sentence Haymond to more time in prison—five years to life.

The question in *Haymond* was straightforward: Under *Alleyne*, can a judge increase a defendant's minimum sentence by finding him guilty by a preponderance of the evidence without the input of a jury? By a 5–4 vote the court said no, finding the statute unconstitutional. In his plurality opinion—joined by Justices Ruth Bader Ginsburg, Sonia Sotomayor, and Elena Kagan—Gorsuch explained that a judge's "authority to issue a sentence derives from, and is limited by, the jury's factual findings of criminal conduct." By forcing judges to exceed that authority, Congress ran afoul of the Constitution.

Breyer concurred in the judgment only. His own brief opinion noted that the law in question was "less like ordinary revocation" of supervised release and "more like punishment for a new offense, to which the jury right would typically attach." Breyer seemed eager to clarify that most supervised release proceedings are consistent with the Fifth and Sixth amendments, but this one strayed too far afield from "the original crime of conviction."

In a furious dissent joined by Roberts, Thomas, and Kavanaugh, Alito wrote that Breyer's narrow concurrence "saved our jurisprudence from the consequences of the plurality opinion, which is not based on the original meaning of the Sixth Amendment, is irreconcilable with precedent, and sports rhetoric with potentially revolutionary implications." Indeed, Alito wrote, Gorsuch's plurality opinion "appears to have been carefully crafted for the purpose of laying the groundwork for later decisions of much broader scope."

"Many passages in the opinion," Alito continued, "suggest that the entire system of supervised release . . . is fundamentally flawed in ways that cannot be fixed." These passages "strongly suggest that the Sixth Amendment right to a jury trial applies to any supervised-release revocation proceeding." And this in turn "means that as a practical matter supervised-release revocation proceedings cannot be held." Alito pointed out that federal courts held 1,809 jury trials in 2018. That same year, by contrast, "they adjudicated 16,946 revocations of supervised release, and there is simply no way that the federal courts could empanel enough juries to adjudicate all those proceedings."

Applying the Sixth Amendment here, Alito concluded, would cause the "whole concept of supervised release" to "come crashing down." He would let judges send offenders back to prison for longer than a jury permitted because they are no longer "the accused" but rather "the convicted." Consequently, any further punishment is "implicitly authorized" by the jury's initial verdict.

It is too soon to tell whether, as Alito wrote, "the whole system of supervised release" is now "like a 40-ton truck speeding down a steep mountain road with no brakes." Breyer's concurrence limited the holding to the facts at hand yet also seemed to endorse key aspects of Gorsuch's logic. If these five justices are willing to enforce the rule laid down in *Haymond*, the supervised release system could be in real peril.

Commentators frequently discuss the Supreme Court as if it were a legislature neatly divided into Republicans and Democrats. That narrative falls apart in these six rulings and is especially inapt when assessing the criminal justice jurisprudence of Trump's nominees. Kavanaugh, by any metric, is a deeply conservative justice, but his opinion in *Flowers* is an unflinching denunciation of prosecutorial racism. Gorsuch has no sympathy for death row inmates or indigent defendants. Yet when the government seeks to evade constitutional safeguards in its drive to secure a conviction, he will zealously apply the Fifth and Sixth Amendments.

Gorsuch's attitude was on display during arguments in *Haymond*, as he grilled Justice Department attorney Eric Feigin about Congress's decision to move from parole to supervised release. "Why doesn't that choice have consequences?" Gorsuch asked Feigin. "And why isn't one of those consequences" that offenders receive a jury trial? "And why is the government so anxious to avoid having the involvement of citizens in this process? . . . Congress self-consciously created this system, and . . . I just don't understand why the government resists the involvement of a jury of a man's or woman's peers."

To the other conservatives, the government is basically trustworthy, at least when it doles out punishments to prisoners. To Gorsuch, the government is a Leviathan that must be brought to heel by vigilant courts.

Progressives have been wary of embracing either Kavanaugh or Gorsuch as an ally on criminal justice—and for good reason. While Gorsuch is devoted to the right of trial by jury, more than 90 percent of defendants in the United States take plea deals. (They may face a longer sentence if convicted at trial.) Moreover, around 80 percent of defendants in the country's most populous counties use public defenders. Gorsuch's jurisprudence would not help the millions of Americans who forgo a jury trial and rely on public defenders.

Still, neither Gorsuch nor Kavanaugh have voted like law-and-order conservatives of decades past. Previous Republican nominees such as Chief Justice Warren Burger voted reliably against criminal defendants in every case; today, Alito and Thomas come closest to fitting that mold. Their new colleagues are more nuanced, building coalitions with the liberals that lead to progressive results. They are, in that sense, aligned with the president who appointed them: in late 2018 Trump signed the First Step Act, a bipartisan criminal justice reform bill that shortened sentences for thousands of offenders.

The U.S. Supreme Court may sometimes operate like a political institution, particularly when it confronts political questions. At its best, though, the court's nine justices grapple earnestly with the demands of constitutional liberty and the limits of government action. They do not always get it right, but a majority of the court has a serious (if sporadically applied) interest in subduing the Leviathan.

Huddled Masses

Immigration, ICE, and Asylum

At a May 2016 campaign event, Donald Trump unleashed his fury on Judge Gonzalo Curiel, who was overseeing a class action lawsuit against Trump University. A number of former students accused the school of fraud, and Curiel had scheduled the case for trial. Trump, then the presumptive Republican presidential nominee, was enraged that Curiel had not thrown out the case.

"We're in front of a very hostile judge," Trump told the crowd. "The judge was appointed by Barack Obama." Trump declared that Curiel "should recuse himself because he's given us ruling after ruling after ruling, negative, negative, negative." Then he added, "What happens is the judge, who happens to be, we believe, Mexican, which is great. I think that's fine."

Trump did not, in fact, think it was "fine." Several days later, he made his critique more explicit in an interview with the *Wall Street Journal*. He told the newspaper that Curiel had "an absolute conflict" in the case because he was "of Mexican heritage," and Trump had pledged to seal off the southern border. "I'm building a wall," Trump said. "It's an inherent conflict of interest." He reiterated this claim in an interview with CNN's Jake Tapper. "We are building a wall. He's a Mexican," Trump told Tapper in reference to Curiel. "I think he should recuse himself."

Gonzago Curiel is not "a Mexican." He is a U.S. citizen who was born in Indiana to Mexican immigrants. Legal analysts universally agreed that none of his rulings evinced a whiff of bias against Trump. Indeed, Curiel successfully persuaded the parties in the Trump University lawsuit to reach a settlement, and in February 2019 the judge rejected a lawsuit attempting to block Trump's efforts to build a border wall.

Yet Trump never retracted his racist attack on Curiel. Instead, Trump doubled down on his strategy of lobbing criticisms at judges who ruled against him. In 2017 Judge James L. Robart halted Trump's first travel ban, which barred citizens of seven Muslim-majority countries from entering the United States. The president dismissed Robart as a "so-called judge" whose ruling was "ridiculous and will [be] overturned!" Early on in his presidency, Trump repeatedly assailed the entire U.S. Court of Appeals for the Ninth Circuit for freezing his policies, berating the court as a "disgrace." In November 2018 when Judge Jon S. Tigar blocked the administration's new policy prohibiting immigrants from applying for asylum if they crossed the southern border illegally, Trump revived his familiar refrain: "This was an Obama judge."

Chief Justice John Roberts remained silent as Trump vilified Curiel and the Ninth Circuit. The president's rebuke of Tigar, however, spurred the chief justice to speak. In 2018 the day before Thanksgiving, Roberts issued an uncharacteristic and extraordinary statement to the Associated Press condemning Trump's comment. "We do not have Obama judges or Trump judges, Bush judges or Clinton judges," the chief justice said. "What we have is an extraordinary group of dedicated judges doing their level best to do equal right to those appearing before them. That independent judiciary is something we should all be thankful for."

Trump shot back, tweeting "Sorry Chief Justice John Roberts, but you do indeed have 'Obama judges,' and they have a much different point of view than the people who are charged with the safety of our country." Roberts did not respond; he had already taken the unprecedented step of issuing a public rejoinder to the president and evidently saw no reason to engage further. In a sense, though, the chief justice still had the last word. One month after Trump's pseudoapology, the Supreme Court issued a 5–4 order keeping the new asylum rule on hold. Roberts sided with the liberal justices, casting the fifth vote against the administration.

The quarrel between Trump and Roberts transformed the asylum case into a clash over the president's power to set immigration policy without a real judicial check. It would later become clear that Roberts had not swung left on immigration but instead seized upon the asylum case to combat the administration's manipulation of the rules in pursuit of a nationalistic agenda. And Roberts's disillusionment would prove incredibly consequential for the term's biggest blockbuster—a fight over the president's ability to add a citizenship question to the 2020 census.

Trump ran for president on a platform of restricting immigration into the United States and removing undocumented immigrations already living here. But like President Barack Obama before him, Trump has failed to persuade Congress to revise the nation's immigration laws. In lieu of a new statute, Trump has relied on his constitutional authority to execute the law, reinterpreting current statutes to curtail the rights of immigrants. His executive actions often rely on strained readings of the law, making them vulnerable to court challenges.

The 2018 Asylum Case

East Bay Sanctuary Covenant v. Trump is a perfect example of this phenomenon. In November 2018, Trump issued a proclamation to address the "mass migration of aliens with no basis for admission into the United States through our southern border." He directed the government to deny asylum to any individual who crosses the U.S.-Mexican border between "ports of entry"—that is, illegally. (A "port of entry" or "port of arrival" is a legal border crossing.) These individuals would no longer be able to claim asylum and could be swiftly deported back to their home countries.

But Trump immediately encountered a roadblock. The Immigration and Nationality Act states that "any alien who is physically present in the United States or who arrives in the United States (whether or not at a designated port of arrival)" may apply for asylum, "irrespective of such alien's status." This provision implements the 1951 Convention Relating to the Status of Refugees, which the United States has ratified. The convention directs signatories not to "impose penalties [on refugees] on account of their illegal entry or presence."

The plain text of the statute is unambiguous: immigrants in the United States are eligible for asylum whether they arrived legally (through a "designated port of arrival") or illegally. To be sure, they do not automatically receive asylum; they must first demonstrate "a well-founded fear of persecution on account of race, religion, nationality, membership in a particular social group, or political opinion." But an immigrant's status should not impair their ability to apply for asylum in the United States.

To work around this rule, the Department of Justice argued that Trump had not barred undocumented immigrations from *applying* for asylum but instead had merely ensured that those who applied would be denied. As a basis for Trump's rule, the department cited a section of the law that allows the government to add "additional limitations and conditions" on asylum so long as they are "consistent with" the statute. The Department of Justice insisted that the new rule was "consistent with" federal law because it did not forbid undocumented immigrants from requesting asylum, only from receiving it.

Tigar rebuffed the Department of Justice's distinction. "The argument strains credulity," he wrote. "To say that one may *apply* for something that one has no right to *receive* is to render the right to apply a dead letter. There simply is no reasonable way to harmonize the two." The president insisted that there was a "crisis" at the southern border, but no emergency could justify disregard for federal law. Tigar therefore issued a nationwide injunction blocking the asylum rule.

A panel of judges for the Ninth Circuit upheld Tigar's decision by a 2–1 vote. Writing for the majority, Judge Jay Bybee—a very conservative George W. Bush appointee—echoed Tigar's logic. "It is the hollowest of rights," Bybee wrote, "that an alien must be allowed to apply for asylum regardless of whether she arrived through a port of entry if another rule makes her categorically ineligible for asylum based on precisely that fact. . . . The technical differences between applying for and eligibility for asylum are of no consequence to a refugee when the bottom line—no possibility of asylum—is the same." He thus blocked the rule under the Administrative Procedure Act, which prohibits agency actions that are "arbitrary and capricious." As Bybee explained, "There surely are enforcement measures that the President and the Attorney General can take to ameliorate the crisis, but continued inaction by Congress is not a sufficient basis under our Constitution for the Executive to rewrite our immigration laws."

The stage was set for a Supreme Court showdown. And Trump had good reason for optimism. In June 2018 the court had upheld the third iteration of the president's travel ban in *Trump v. Hawaii*, which barred citizens of seven countries—including five Muslim-majority nations—from entering the United States. Roberts's opinion cited a statute that allows the president to "suspend the entry" of "any class of aliens" who are "detrimental to the interests of the United States." The chief justice deferred to Trump's finding that individuals covered by the ban posed a threat to national security, even though the government provided minimal evidence to support that rationale. The Trump administration seems to have hoped that Roberts would apply this extreme deference to its asylum rule by interpreting "additional limitations and conditions" to mean anything the president wants.

Roberts declined to adopt the government's view this time around. When the administration asked his court to lift Tigar's injunction, the chief justice, joined by the liberals, refused. Justices Clarence Thomas, Samuel Alito, Neil Gorsuch, and Brett Kavanaugh dissented, indicating that they would have stayed the injunction and allowed the rule to take effect. As is customary, none of the justices wrote separately to explain their reasoning.

Why did Roberts vote the way he did in *East Bay Sanctuary Covenant*? The most obvious answer is that he agreed with Bybee that Tigar was correct: Trump's rule would render immigrants' right to request asylum "a dead letter," contravening Congress's command. The more complicated question is whether Roberts's spat with the president factored into his decision. After all, Trump criticized Tigar for issuing an injunction *in this very case*; if Roberts had voted to lift that injunction, he would have implicitly agreed with the president that Tigar got it wrong. The president might have gloated that despite Roberts's protests, he ultimately sided against the "Obama judge."

Whatever the motivation behind Roberts's vote, it marked a turning point in the chief justice's relationship with the administration. In *Hawaii*, Roberts's sweeping opinion had hinted that the conservative majority would tolerate Trump's excesses and misrepresentations. The chief justice's vote in *East Bay Sanctuary Covenant* indicated that his deference to the president had a limit. Roberts's impatience with the Trump administration would have dramatic repercussions in the census case six months later.

If progressive advocates thought that the chief justice had abandoned his conservative approach to immigrants' rights, though, they would soon be disappointed. The court contended with another major immigration case in O.T. 2018, *Nielsen v. Preap*, that resulted in a 5–4 decision along the usual ideological lines. *Preap* placed the court at the center of a major public controversy: the powers of Immigration and Customs Enforcement (ICE), a federal law enforcement agency tasked with detaining and deporting undocumented immigrants. Roberts and his conservative colleagues have shown no interest in curbing those powers.

Preap revolved around a statute that requires the mandatory detention, without bond, of certain undocumented immigrants. (Most immigrants can be released on bond if they show that they are not a danger or a flight risk.) One provision states that immigration officials "shall take into custody" any undocumented immigrant who has committed a certain criminal offense "when the alien is released" from jail. (Qualifying offenses include drug violations, aggravated felonies, and crimes of "moral turpitude," a capacious category that encompasses minor crimes such as stealing bus transfers.)

The Trump administration claimed that under this provision, ICE may arrest undocumented immigrants a day, a month, a decade, or even a half century after they have been released from custody—then hold them indefinitely. The American Civil Liberties Union (ACLU), which represented the plaintiffs, argued that ICE can only detain these individuals without bond if it intercepts them *immediately* upon their release from jail. If ICE fails to do so, the ACLU asserted, it may still detain them later on. But ICE must grant them the same bond hearings that other individuals in immigrant detention receive.

Preap came down to the meaning of "when." The Trump administration asserted that the word grants the government an open-ended option to lock up this class of immigrants at any point. By contrast, the ACLU believed that the word conveys a sense of "immediacy." The ACLU argued that the purpose of the statute was to prevent a "gap" between an undocumented immigrant's release from criminal custody and her or his transfer to immigrant detention. Two courts of appeals sided with the ACLU's interpretation; four others sided with the government's.

In an opinion by Justice Samuel Alito, the Supreme Court's conservatives ruled for the administration. Alito wrote that the word "when" only clarifies that ICE cannot "cut short an alien's state prison sentence in order to usher him more easily right into immigration detention." The term also exhorts ICE "to act quickly" once an undocumented immigrant is freed but does not require speed or immediacy. This means that ICE can wait years to detain immigrants who have completed their sentences, and once ICE arrests an immigrant, it can still deny that person a bond hearing.

To Breyer, who dissented along with his liberal colleagues, this reasoning led to an unconstitutional result. "The issue may sound technical," he acknowledged. "But it is extremely important" because it implicates "the long-standing right of virtually all persons to receive a bail hearing." Breyer wrote that the word "when" requires ICE to act "within a reasonable time" after an immigrant is freed from jail. He defined "a reasonable time" as six months, citing an earlier Supreme Court decision that interpreted "when" to create a "presumptive 6-month limit." If ICE waits any longer than six months to detain an immigrant, Breyer wrote, it must offer that person a bond hearing.

Preap was a difficult case. Neither the majority nor the dissent put forth an airtight interpretation of the (inartful and confusing) law in question. The plain text of the statute seems to convey some urgency but does not identify a six-month time limit. Breyer sought to impose this deadline to square the law with the demands of due process. The court "cannot interpret the words of this specific statute," he wrote, "without also considering basic promises that America's legal system has long made to all persons." He continued:

> We cannot decide that question without bearing in mind basic American legal values: the Government's duty not to deprive any "person" of "liberty" without "due process of law." ... I would have thought that Congress meant to adhere to these values and did not intend to allow the Government to apprehend persons years after their release from prison and hold them indefinitely without a bail hearing. In my view, the Court should interpret the words of this statute to reflect Congress' likely intent, an intent that is consistent with our basic values.

"I fear," he concluded, that the court's decision "will work serious harm to the principles for which American law has long stood."

Alito's decision in *Preap* built upon his opinion in 2018's *Jennings v. Rodriguez.* A similar case, *Jennings* involved the government's ability to detain certain immigrants, including asylum seekers, indefinitely. Alito, joined by his fellow conservatives, ruled that federal law authorizes the government to hold these individuals without bond while it adjudicates their claims. In dissent, Breyer warned that the majority had undermined the "ancient and important right" of freedom from "arbitrary detention."

It would be a mistake to view *Jennings* or *Preap* exclusively as vehicles for Trump's agenda. Both cases originated during Obama's presidency, and the Justice Department took its prodetention position under Attorney General Loretta Lynch. The outcome in *Preap* may be a boon to Trump, who has empowered ICE to aggressively detain undocumented immigrants who pose no threat to the community. But it was not a political decision. As a matter of statutory interpretation, Alito's opinion is plausible if debatable—it tried to make sense of the law and implement it as Congress intended.

Trump's asylum rule was an entirely different beast. It is difficult to understand how Thomas, Alito, Gorsuch, and Kavanaugh could vote to let the policy take effect when it directly contradicted the letter of the law—difficult, that is, without resorting to cynicism about the conservative justices' motives. It is one thing to say that courts must apply an immigration law as Congress wrote it even though it is harsh; it is quite another thing to say that the president can ignore an immigration law as Congress wrote it even though it is generous. Trump seems to have four solid votes to uphold his administration's actions no matter how flagrantly illegal they might appear.

The chief justice's approach to immigration cases is more consistent. Roberts's votes in *East Bay Sanctuary Covenant* and *Preap* might seem to be at odds, but they are actually harmonious. In both cases, the chief justice tried to respect Congress's primacy in promulgating immigration law. His vote against Trump's asylum policy adhered to that principle—with the added benefit of reminding the president that the Supreme Court is not a mere "outpost of the executive branch," as *The Atlantic*'s Garrett Epps put it. Roberts is willing to let the Trump administration pursue conservative policy. But when the administration tries to stretch the law too far, the chief justice just might snap.

Chapter 6

Big Business Before the Bar

The Roberts Court has been a great friend to big business. Since Chief Justice John Roberts and Justice Samuel Alito joined the U.S. Supreme Court in 2005 and 2006, respectively, the court has consistently sided with the U.S. Chamber of Commerce, a conservative lobbying group that represents corporate interests. The chamber files dozens of amicus briefs each term urging the court to adopt its stance on the law. According to a study by the Constitutional Accountability Center, a progressive think tank and law firm, the Roberts Court has ruled for the chamber's position in 70 percent of cases. The five conservative justices are substantially more likely than the four liberals to take the side of the Chamber of Commerce.

When progressive critics of the Supreme Court such as Democratic senator Sheldon Whitehouse accuse it of "corporate capture," they are describing this phenomenon: five Republican-appointed justices continually side with a lobbying group that spends millions of dollars electing Republican lawmakers and judges each year. The Chamber of Commerce's winning streak does not necessarily mean that its amicus briefs have swayed the justices to the right; it simply indicates that a majority of the court is aligned with the chamber's ideology.

In the 2016–2017 term, the Chamber of Commerce's win rate soared to 80 percent. In the 2017–2018 term it crept even higher, up to 90 percent. The most recent term seemed poised to continue that trend. Per the Constitutional Accountability Center, the Supreme Court heard twenty-four cases in which the chamber weighed in. In twenty-two of those cases, the lower court ruled against the position favored by business. It appeared that the Roberts Court was preparing to reverse these decisions, issuing its usual procession of probusiness rulings.

Then something strange happened: the U.S. Chamber of Commerce saw its win rate plummet. By the end of the term, the chamber was on the winning side of just 57 percent of the court's rulings. Moreover, this win rate is inflated by a Pyrrhic victory for the chamber in *Merck v. Albrecht*, in which the court ruled for business on a technical matter and then made it easier for patients to sue drug manufacturers under state law. Counting *Albrecht* as a loss for business, the chamber's success rate as amici dropped to a historic low at the Roberts Court this term.

The Chamber of Commerce's nosedive at the Supreme Court should not be mistaken for a permanent turn against business. Roberts and his conservative colleagues remain strong allies of the business community; O.T. 2018 will probably be an outlier, and it is safe to expect the chamber's win rate to shoot back up in the near future. But a trio of decisions in 2019—*New Prime v. Oliveira, Apple v. Pepper*, and *Home Depot v. Jackson*—illustrate how consumers and employees can occasionally prevail at this procorporate court.

New Prime v. Oliveira

In 1925, Congress passed the Federal Arbitration Act (FAA) to govern disagreements between commercial enterprises. At the time, many federal courts declined to enforce arbitration agreements, which required parties to settle their disputes out of court before an arbiter instead of a judge. Congress intended that the FAA would extinguish judicial hostility to arbitration when businesses believed that the process would be superior to a court battle.

For decades, the FAA played a modest role in contractual disputes between merchants. Then in the 1980s, a group of corporate attorneys recognized that the law could be deployed more strategically. Virtually every scholar to study the law has concluded that it was intended never to apply to disputes involving employees and consumers or to state courts. But the language of the FAA is quite broad: it declares that arbitration agreements are "valid, irrevocable, and enforceable." Corporate lawyers therefore advised their clients that they could avoid both individual and class action lawsuits by slipping individual arbitration agreements into their contracts. Consumers and employees would have to settle their claims one by one in arbitration. The company could choose the location, the arbiter, and the procedures.

This arbitration revolution was led in part by a corporate defense attorney named John G. Roberts Jr. It took a while for Roberts and his allies to convince the Supreme

Chapter 6

Court to adopt their rather radical interpretation of the statute. Indeed, by the time the court enshrined a sweeping view of the FAA into law, Roberts was serving as chief justice. In 2011's *AT&T Mobility v. Concepcion*, the five conservative justices ruled that states must allow corporations to force consumers into individual arbitration. In 2013's *American Express Co. v. Italian Colors Restaurant*, the same justices ruled that courts must enforce individual arbitration clauses even when the cost of individual arbitration exceeds potential recovery.

These decisions allowed a range of corporations—credit card companies, cell phone carriers, cable and Internet providers, online retailers, car rental companies, nursing homes, and so on—to force customers out of court and into individual arbitration. Few customers pursue this route, and those who do rarely receive a meaningful monetary award. A 2015 study by the *New York Times* found that roughly two-thirds of consumers who contest credit card fraud, fees, or loans get zero dollars in arbitration. As the *New York Times* explained, "the rules of arbitration largely favor companies, which can even steer cases to friendly arbitrators."

Mandatory arbitration has also crept into employment contracts. In 2017 the Economic Policy Institute, a progressive think tank, found that more than 55 percent of non-union private-sector workers are bound by these clauses. The Supreme Court accelerated their proliferation in 2018's *Epic Systems v. Lewis*. In that case, the software company Epic Systems asked the court to enforce the FAA against workers who filed a class action lawsuit for wage theft.

These workers encountered a problem. In 2014, Epic Systems sent an e-mail to every employee stating that all employees would be subject to mandatory individual arbitration. "I understand that if I continue to work at Epic," the statement read, "I will be deemed to have accepted this Agreement." Workers had two choices: agree or quit.

In litigation, Epic System's employees claimed that this mandatory arbitration agreement violated the National Labor Relations Act (NLRA) of 1935. A landmark piece of New Deal legislation, the NLRA allows workers to take collective action to safeguard their interests. Section 7 of the law grants them the right to engage in "concerted activities for the purpose of collective bargaining or other mutual aid or protection." Epic System's employees argued that class action lawsuits constituted "concerted activities" for their "mutual aid or protection." Thus, the NLRA should trump the FAA.

In a 5–4 decision, the Supreme Court disagreed. Justice Neil Gorsuch, joined by the other conservatives, dismissed Section 7—which was meant to be American labor's Magna Carta—as a "mousehole." Gorsuch read the NLRA as protecting only "organization and collective bargaining" as well as "closely related" activities such as picketing. He repeatedly referred to Epic System's mandatory arbitration rule as an "agreement" between "employees and employers," even though workers had no real choice but to accept it. Justice Ruth Bader Ginsburg's dissent castigated the majority for authorizing "take-it-or-leave-it labor contracts harking back to the type called 'yellow dog.'" (These contracts forbade employees from joining a union.) In a statement read from the bench, Ginsburg called on Congress "to correct the court's elevation of the [FAA] over workers' right to act in concern."

Epic Systems sparked an immense backlash. Critics, including Ginsburg, charged the majority with reviving the so-called *Lochner* era, when the court relied on "freedom of contract" to invalidate business regulations, including minimum wage and maximum hour rules. They also pointed out that the court's logic could be used to block discrimination claims that require proof of mistreatment on a group-wide basis. Was any employment law safe from the FAA's reach after *Epic Systems*?

Dominic Oliveira put that question to the test in *New Prime*. Oliveira worked as a driver for New Prime, a trucking company. When he began work, he was required to complete 10,000 miles hauling freight for New Prime—for free, as an "apprentice." He was then compelled to complete another 30,000 miles as a "trainee," for which he was paid about $4 an hour. Once he became a full-fledged driver, Oliveira was designated as a contractor rather than an employee. He was forced to lease his own truck (from a company owned by the owners of New Prime), buy his own equipment (from the New Prime store), and pay for his own gas, often from New Prime gas pumps.

Because New Prime classified Oliveira as an "independent contractor," it deducted the costs from his paycheck. Sometimes that paycheck wound up negative due to these deductions, meaning that New Prime essentially charged Oliveira to work for the company.

In 2015, Oliveira filed a class action lawsuit on behalf of himself and tens of thousands of other "contractors." He alleged that New Prime had misclassified him as a contractor to underpay him, a violation of federal labor law. But Oliveira's contract with the company declared that all disputes must be resolved through individual arbitration, a process that is costly, time-consuming, and unjust, favoring employers over workers. New Prime asserted that under the FAA, courts must enforce this "agreement" and dismiss Oliveira's claims.

Broad as the FAA's language may be, though, it expressly *excludes* "contracts of employment of . . . workers engaged in . . . interstate commerce," such as "seamen" and "railroad employees." Everyone agrees that truckers qualify for this exception, but New Prime asserted that truckers who work as contractors do not have "contracts of employment" and thus do not qualify. And by classifying so many workers as contractors, the company believed that it had worked around the FAA's exemption.

In light of *Epic Systems*, Oliveira seemed to be careening toward a 5–4 loss at the Supreme Court. But in a staggering turn of events, the court ruled *unanimously* in his favor in January 2019. And the decision was penned by Gorsuch himself. (Justice Brett Kavanaugh did not participate, as he had not joined the court in time for oral arguments.)

When Congress passed the FAA in 1925, Gorsuch explained, "Dictionaries tended to treat 'employment' more or less as a synonym for 'work.'" In fact, "all work was treated as employment," whether or not "a formal employer-employee or master-servant relationship" existed. Citing six dictionaries from the era as well as contemporaneous statutes and rulings, Gorsuch concluded that "contract of employment" was understood to encompass "work agreements involving independent contractors." As a result, Oliveira, along with other truckers and transportation contractors, qualified for the FAA's exemption. His class action lawsuit could proceed in court.

Parts of Gorsuch's opinion in *New Prime* read like a response to Ginsburg's dissent in *Epic Systems*. The court, he insisted, would not "squeeze more from the statute's text" than it allowed. To the liberal justices, of course, the court had done just that in *Epic Systems*. But Gorsuch's textualist take on *New Prime* placed a limit on the FAA's judicial expansion. The court will continue to give the FAA a sweeping effect in most industry sectors; transportation workers, however, will retain their right to sue collectively.

In a second arbitration decision issued in April, *Lamps Plus v. Varela*, the conservative justices confirmed that *New Prime* did not mark a turn away from FAA precedent. By a 5–4 vote, the majority held in *Lamps Plus* that courts cannot compel class-wide arbitration when a contract is "ambiguous" about its availability. (Class-wide arbitration allows individuals to bring their claims collectively before an arbiter, a more effective and convenient process than bringing them one-by-one.) Lamps Plus, a California light fixture company, had drafted a contract that implied the availability of class-wide arbitration for its employees but did not explicitly confirm it. Roberts's majority opinion held that under the FAA, such an "ambiguous" agreement does not permit class-wide arbitration.

The decision in *Lamps Plus* was a startling intrusion into state contract law. All fifty states apply a rule that ambiguous contracts must be construed against the drafter. Because Lamps Plus wrote the contract here, California law would resolve the ambiguity in favor of employees. In other words, the state's antidrafter rule would require the company to accept class-wide arbitration. But as Justice Elena Kagan wrote in her dissent, the majority had used the FAA to "federalize basic contract law," replacing the antidrafter rule with a proarbitration standard. Every other liberal justice wrote a dissent as well, each underscoring their own frustration with Roberts's opinion.

It did not matter to the conservative majority. *New Prime* was an anomaly, and *Lamps Plus* is the norm. At the Roberts Court, arbitration reigns supreme.

Apple v. Pepper

At a 2017 conference about American monopolies, Judge Richard Posner, a giant of antitrust law, shocked audiences with a dismissive declaration: "Antitrust is dead, isn't it? That was my impression."

Posner was exaggerating but not by much. In 2017, antitrust enforcement was in a decrepit state. President Barack Obama's administration had done little to halt rapid market concentration, allowing a few major players to dominate the economy. As David Dayen pointed out in *The Nation* that year, there were four major cable and Internet providers, four major commercial banks, four major airlines, and four major technology companies—Amazon, Facebook, Apple, and Google. Although President Donald Trump's administration has stepped up antitrust enforcement, its efforts have not borne much fruit. The Justice Department's attempt to block the merger between AT&T and Time Warner failed in court. Concentration continues apace.

Courts played an important part in the hobbling of antitrust. As Dayen noted, a group of academics known as the Chicago School effectively rewrote antimonopoly statutes in the 1970s and 1980s "without altering a word" of federal law. The Chicago School, which included Posner, persuaded the courts that antitrust laws were intended to benefit "consumer welfare," not merely encourage competition. If corporations engaged in anticompetitive behavior without harming consumers by raising prices, this theory proclaimed, their stranglehold on the market posed no antitrust problem.

At the same time that courts adopted this theory, they made it more difficult for consumers who *were* harmed to sue monopolists. Federal law allows "any person" who is "injured" by antitrust violations to file suit and "recover threefold the damages by him sustained," in addition to attorneys' fees. Granting victims the right to threefold (or "treble") damages is strong medicine. But in 1977's *Illinois Brick v. Illinois*, the Supreme Court prohibited lawsuits by "indirect purchasers"—that is, consumers who do not buy *directly* from an alleged antitrust violator. Under this rule, customers who purchase goods from an intermediary —who in turn bought those goods from a monopolist—cannot sue the monopolist for damages even though the intermediary "passed on the overcharge" to customers.

Like so much antitrust jurisprudence, *Illinois Brick* was based less on the text of a statute than on economic theory. The court feared that proving "indirect-purchaser" damages would be "virtually unascertainable" because of the "extremely complex issues" involved. Calculating and proving these damages, the court speculated, would impose excess "costs to the judicial system and the efficient enforcement of the antitrust laws."

In light of this historical backdrop, the plaintiffs in *Apple v. Pepper* had a steep hill to climb. Their case began in 2011, when they sued Apple for allegedly monopolizing the retail market for apps. Under the current system, independent developers create apps and then contract with Apple, which sells them through its App Store. To place an app in the store, developers must pay Apple $99 each year as well as a 30 percent commission on every app sale. Unlike Android users, who can download apps from anywhere, Apple users *must* buy apps from the App Store. The *Pepper* plaintiffs alleged that Apple had locked iPhone owners "into buying apps only from Apple and paying Apple's 30% fee" even if they want "to buy apps elsewhere or pay less."

These plaintiffs quickly crashed into the wall of *Illinois Brick*. A district court held that they were not direct purchasers from Apple because developers, not Apple, set the app price. The U.S. Court of Appeals for the Ninth Circuit reversed, ruling that the plaintiffs were obviously direct purchasers since they bought the apps from Apple. This permitted the lawsuit to proceed. When the Supreme Court agreed to review the Ninth Circuit's ruling, it seemed like an ominous sign for the plaintiffs. Would the justices expand *Illinois Brick* to let tech titans maintain their own "walled gardens" and take a cut of every app purchase?

During oral arguments, Justice Brett Kavanaugh indicated discomfort with Apple's theory—and *Illinois Brick*. He questioned Solicitor General Noel Francisco, who weighed in on Apple's side, over "ambiguity about what *Illinois Brick* means here." If that ambiguity exists, Kavanaugh asked, shouldn't it "be resolved by looking at the text of the state? 'Any person injured.' That's broad."

Kavanaugh's questions weren't a feint. In May he authored a 5–4 decision, joined by the liberal justices, allowing the lawsuit to move forward. The iPhone users, he wrote, are "direct purchasers" who were "injured" by

Apple's alleged monopoly. "That straightforward conclusion," Kavanaugh explained, "follows from the text of the antitrust laws and from our precedents." He cast *Illinois Brick* as a "bright-line rule": a customer who buys a product from an alleged monopolist can file suit, while a customer who buys a product from an "intermediary" cannot.

"There is no intermediary in the distribution chain between Apple and the consumer," Kavanaugh concluded. "The iPhone owners purchase apps directly from the retailer Apple, who is the alleged antitrust violator. The iPhone owners pay the alleged overcharge directly to Apple." As a result, they can sue Apple. *Illinois Brick* cannot serve as "a get-out-of-court-free card."

Gorsuch wrote a dissent, joined by Roberts, Thomas, and Alito. Although Gorsuch had questioned the wisdom of *Illinois Brick* during oral arguments, he rose to its defense in his searing opinion. He praised its "ancient and venerable" notion of "economic reality" and criticized Kavanaugh for "whittling it away to a bare formalism." Gorsuch suggested that the majority "just disagrees with *Illinois Brick*" and wanted to replace it with "an easily manipulated and formalistic rule."

The dueling opinions in *Pepper* by Kavanaugh and Gorsuch revealed a fundamental disagreement over antitrust. Gorsuch plainly shares the Chicago School's belief that corporations will operate fairly without antitrust oversight. His dissent dwelt on the consequences of *Pepper* for businesses, complaining that it might force them to "abandon their preferred—and presumably more efficient—distribution arrangements." Kavanaugh, by contrast, focused on consumers and the harms that monopolists can pass onto them under the guise of efficiency. Many happy iPhone users find the App Store adequate and easy to use. But is Apple exploiting this "walled garden" to stifle competition? To Kavanaugh, discontented iPhone users deserve to make their case in court. The plain text of the law grants them that right.

These plaintiffs are still at the beginning of their fight. They must now prove a true antitrust violation and demonstrate damages, which will require years of litigation. But thanks to Kavanaugh, they have surmounted their first obstacle. For years, the Supreme Court's conservatives have cast a jaundiced eye toward antitrust suits, assuming that free market principles would preserve competition without government interference. Kavanaugh's opinion in *Pepper* may presage a more vigorous approach to antitrust.

Home Depot v. Jackson

The story of *Home Depot* is a tale of greed, grift, and civil procedure and centers on a scheme that involved three companies: Home Depot, Citibank, and Carolina Water Systems Inc. Here is how it allegedly worked. Representatives from Home Depot or CWS called homeowners and claimed that "contaminants" were found in nearby tap water. They urged homeowners to let them perform a test for "contaminants," which was really just a test for water hardness; almost all tap water tested positive, even if it was perfectly safe. But CWS told homeowners that the positive result proved their water was unsafe and required a $9,000 water purification system. (It did not mention that other companies sell the same system for $1,400.) The company then told homeowners that they had been approved for a Home Depot–branded Citibank credit card, which they could use to pay for the system with deferred interest.

George Jackson got suckered into this alleged scam and, like many others, could not afford to pay off the charges he put on the credit card to pay for the overpriced water purification system. A company representative allegedly told Jackson that the Citibank card had zero interest for two years—but the interest rate jumped to 25.99 percent after one year. Jackson could not afford to pay, so Citibank sued him in state court to collect the debt. Eventually he secured the representation of consumer protection lawyers who filed a counterclaim against Citibank as well as class action claims against Home Depot and CWS on behalf of about 290 other homeowners targeted by the alleged scam. He claimed that the companies, working together, had violated North Carolina laws prohibiting unfair and deceptive trade practices.

Home Depot promptly tried to move the case from a North Carolina court to federal court—a typical corporate tactic, since federal courts are widely considered to be more business-friendly than state courts. Most federal judges are former prosecutors or corporate attorneys; by comparison, many state courts judges previously worked as plaintiffs' lawyers, representing employees or consumers against corporations. State courts, as a result, are considered much friendlier to consumer class actions.

Republican Party lawmakers also think that state courts are too favorable toward class actions, which is why the Republican-controlled Congress passed the Class Action Fairness Act (CAFA) in 2005. In his definitive study of the law, Edward A. Purcell Jr. described CAFA as "the product of an extended and well-organized political campaign" led by, among others, the U.S. Chamber of Commerce. The act marked an effort to "limit corporate liability and weaken or deny judicial remedies to those harmed by corporate business." CAFA expanded corporate defendants' ability to remove class actions rooted in state law from state to federal court, where they had a better chance of winning. In response to Jackson's claims, Home Depot argued that CAFA allowed it to move the entire case out of North Carolina courts and get it before a federal judge.

But Home Depot hit a snag. Under a long line of cases going back to the 1940s, only a *defendant* can move a case from state to federal court. And a defendant is defined as the party sued by the original plaintiff. Here, Jackson is the defendant; remember, Citibank sued him to collect the debt he owed—that is how the whole case started. Under the usual rules, then, Home Depot cannot escape North Carolina courts.

Home Depot tried to wriggle out from under this issue by arguing that CAFA changed everything with a single word: "any." The law states that "any defendant" can move a case to federal court. And according to Home Depot, the word changed the long-standing definition of "defendant" to encompass third parties slapped with a counterclaim. By adding just one word, Home Depot argued, CAFA upended nearly eighty years of law, granting corporations facing class action counterclaims a new right to move cases into federal court.

The Supreme Court rejected this argument in a 5–4 decision, with Justice Clarence Thomas joining the liberals and writing for the court. Nothing in CAFA, Thomas explained, altered the well-established "limitation on who can remove, which suggests that Congress intended to leave that limit in place." By adding the word "any," Congress "did not expand the types of parties eligible to remove a class action." Instead, Congress altered an old rule that a case can only be moved to federal court if "all defendants" consent, granting "any defendant" the ability to move a case. But because Home Depot is not a defendant under the law, it still has no right to move the case to federal court.

In his lengthy dissent joined by the other conservatives, Justice Samuel Alito wrote that the majority's conclusion "subverts CAFA's evident aims" by creating a "loophole." His opinion focused on CAFA's history, noting Congress's skepticism toward class actions, state courts, and "the plaintiffs' bar." Alito would have read CAFA to further the law's "purpose" and "policy" of "help[ing] class-action defendants avoid" state courts, where judges may be "biased."

There are two curious aspects to Alito's dissent. First, every conservative justice identifies to some degree with "textualism," a mode of statutory interpretation that focuses on a statute's plain text rather than its legislative purpose. Yet Alito's opinion dwells extensively on CAFA's purpose, rendering the law's language an afterthought. Second, the dissent reads like a majority opinion. It is more than twice as long as the actual majority opinion and comes across like a statement of the law rather than a rebuttal to Thomas. Several court watchers even speculated on Twitter that Alito's dissent was originally a majority opinion. Under this theory, Thomas initially sided with the conservatives, then switched his vote after realizing how far Alito had strayed from the law's text.

Whether or not Thomas flipped behind the scenes, his opinion marked a rare triumph for class action lawsuits at the Supreme Court. George Jackson must still prove his case before a North Carolina judge, but the deck will not be stacked against him. Thomas remains a deeply conservative judge whose decisions almost always favor business over consumers. But in *Home Depot*, his textualist methodology led to a surprisingly progressive outcome.

Textualism is the link between *New Prime*, *Pepper*, and *Home Depot*. Using the U.S. Chamber of Commerce's position as a proxy for conservatism, business should have won all three cases. By most metrics, after all, this court is very far to the right; its median justice, Roberts, is significantly more conservative than his predecessors in the center. Really, Roberts is not a centrist or a swing voter in the traditional meaning of either term. As we will see, his votes with the liberal bloc in O.T. 2018 were more strategic than ideological, driven by institutional concerns about the role of the court in American politics.

And yet, during its first term without a bona fide swing voter, the Supreme Court swung against the Chamber of Commerce and its allies over and over again. The common thread that runs through these three cases as well as others that went against the chamber's position is textualism. In *New Prime*, the court emphasized the words "contract of employment," in *Pepper* "any person injured," and in *Home Depot* "any defendant." Textualism is sometimes derided as inherently conservative, but in each case here the winning party snatched a liberal victory by zeroing in on a few key words.

It would be naive to assume that progressives can always win at the Supreme Court when they make the better textualist argument. Sometimes the five conservative justices appear determined to side with business interests and ignore the realities of the workplace; consider, for instance, Gorsuch's risible claim in *Epic Systems* that mandatory arbitration provisions are voluntary "agreements" freely entered into by employees. For every *New Prime*, there is a *Lamps Plus*. Still, the three cases discussed in this chapter show how liberal advocates can beat their corporate counterparts in business cases. They may face an uphill battle—but with the law on their side, they just might prevail.

Chapter 7

Gunning for the Administrative State

During oral arguments in *Gundy v. United States*, Justice Neil Gorsuch name-dropped an unlikely ally: the American Civil Liberties Union (ACLU). Gorsuch asked Jeffrey Wall, the principal deputy solicitor general, to respond to an argument in the ACLU's amicus brief on behalf of Herman Gundy, a sex offender challenging a federal registration law. Days before the ACLU announced its opposition to Brett Kavanaugh's nomination, a rare move for an organization that typically refrains from endorsing or opposing judicial nominees. In 2017, the group issued a sharply critical report on Gorsuch—who, upon joining the bench, promptly ruled against the ACLU in a series of high-profile cases. Yet here was Gorsuch, relying on the ACLU's reasoning to challenge the authority of the federal government to impose retroactive penalties on sex offenders.

Gorsuch no doubt has a civil libertarian streak that sometimes proves helpful for criminal defendants. His hostility toward the law in *Gundy*, however, had less to do with sex offender registries than with the "administrative state"—those federal agencies that interpret and enforce congressional statutes. In two cases in O.T. 2018, *Gundy* and *Kisor v. Wilkie*, Gorsuch sought to radically reduce the role these agencies play in governing the nation. He did not succeed, but he did not quite fail either. Instead, he and several conservatives laid the groundwork for a judicial attack on the "administrative state" that may well carry the day in the near future.

The first case, *Gundy*, revolved around a statute known as the Sex Offender Registration and Notification Act (SORNA). Passed in 2006, SORNA established a national sex offender registry and compelled convicted offenders to register with state officials. Those who fail to register or update their whereabouts face ten years' imprisonment. The law expressly applies to everyone convicted after its passage. But what about the roughly 500,000 people convicted of a sex offense before SORNA? Here the statute was hazy, stating that the attorney general "shall have the authority to specify" its retroactive application and "prescribe rules" for these pre-SORNA offenders. (Every attorney general has applied the law retroactively.)

Herman Gundy committed a sex offense pre-SORNA and was convicted for failing to register under the law. In turn, he challenged SORNA's retroactivity provision as a violation of the "nondelegation doctrine," the principle that Congress cannot shift too much legislative power to another branch of government. The U.S. Supreme Court has deployed this principle only twice in history to knock down federal statutes, both times in 1935 to rein in the New Deal. Today it is moribund, because it only requires Congress to lay out an "intelligible principle" to guide an agency's exercise of authority. The court has held that a law directing Congress to regulate in "the public interest, convenience, or necessity" meets this standard. It is a very easy test to pass. Yet Gundy claimed that SORNA's retroactivity provision flunks it.

Progressives generally defend Congress's authority to delegate broad power to federal agencies. Regulators such as the Environmental Protection Agency (EPA) rely on capacious statutes to carry out their work even when the rest of the government is gridlocked. *Gundy* involved a clash of principles, pitting support for the administrative state against criminal justice reform. The case rallied to Gundy's side a motley crew of organizations, from the liberal ACLU to the libertarian Cato Institute to the Conservative Legal Defense and Education Fund. Each group signed amicus briefs urging the Supreme Court to strike down SORNA's retroactivity clause, though they had very different reasons for doing so. The conservatives and libertarians wanted a sweeping decision that would shrink the scope of government; the ACLU wanted a pinpoint strike against a stringent sex offender law.

By citing the ACLU's amicus brief, Gorsuch conveyed the cross-ideological discomfort with SORNA's retroactivity provision. He asked Wall to respond to the ACLU's argument that the government's position places no real limit on the attorney general's ability to penalize sex offenders however he sees fit. And at one point Gorsuch gave a lecture to Sarah Baumbartel, who represented Gundy, essentially explaining why she should win.

"I'm having trouble thinking of another delegation in which this Court has ever allowed the chief prosecutor of the United States to write the criminal law for those he's going to prosecute," Gorsuch told Baumbartel. "We say that vague criminal laws must be stricken. We've just repeated that last term. What's vaguer than a blank check to the Attorney General of the United States to determine who he's going to prosecute?"

"That's your argument stated very concisely," Justice Ruth Bader Ginsburg quipped to Baumbartel, prompting laughter in the courtroom—though Gorsuch did not crack a smile.

Gundy was argued in early October, just before Kavanaugh joined the bench. As the months passed by, though, no decision was forthcoming. Court watchers speculated that the justices were scrambling to avoid a 4–4 split, which would affirm Gundy's conviction without establishing precedent. The average time between oral arguments and a ruling this term was 105 days, according to Adam Feldman of Empirical SCOTUS, which conducts statistical analysis of the court. So, 105 days after oral arguments, there was no opinion in *Gundy*; 200 days passed, no *Gundy*; then 250 days passed, and still no *Gundy*. By this point the term was winding to a close, with no opinion in a case argued during its first week. If the case had tied 4–4, why was it taking so long to announce the deadlock?

Finally, after 261 one days the court released its opinion in *Gundy*. It was, Feldman noted, the third-longest amount of time in history for any decision in a case argued in the same term. And it was not immediately apparent why deliberations dragged on for so long. The court upheld SORNA's retroactivity provision in a 5–3 vote. The plurality opinion for the four liberals, written by Justice Elena Kagan, pointed out that SORNA's text requires the establishment of "a comprehensive national system for the registration of [sex] offenders" that "includes offenders who committed their offenses before the Act became law." By its own terms, SORNA encompasses any "individual who was convicted of a sex offense"—not just offenders going forward but everybody up to that point too.

"Reasonably read," Kagan wrote, "the Attorney General's role ... was important but limited: It was to apply SORNA to pre-Act offenders as soon as he thought it feasible to do so." And that he did—217 days, to be precise, after SORNA's enactment, Attorney General Alberto R. Gonzales applied the law retroactively.

Kagan found the "intelligible principle" required by the nondelegation doctrine: Congress declared that it wanted SORNA applied retroactively when the attorney general decided it would be practicable to do so. "That delegation," she wrote, "easily passes constitutional muster." And, she pointed out, "if SORNA's delegation is unconstitutional, then most of Government is unconstitutional—dependent as Congress is on the need to give discretion to executive officials to implement its programs."

Justice Samuel Alito provided the fifth vote to uphold the law but did so begrudgingly. "If a majority of this Court were willing to reconsider the approach we have taken for the past 84 years," Alito explained, "I would support that effort. But because a majority is not willing to do that, it would be freakish to single out the provision at issue here for special treatment."

Gorsuch penned a dissent scorning "a plurality of an eight-member Court" for ignoring "the Constitution's demands." Joined by Chief Justice John Roberts and Justice Clarence Thomas, Gorsuch provided a lengthy history lesson about the separation of powers' protection of individual liberty and condemned the "intelligible principle" rule as a "misadventure." He would demand much more, requiring Congress to give the executive branch vastly more guidance in enforcing statutes. Under Gorsuch's standard, federal agencies would be limited to making "factual findings" using "criteria" and "policy judgments" set out by Congress.

This approach would work a revolution in federal law. Hundreds of statutes task the executive branch with some broad goal, then let agencies fill in the details. (Most major agencies lie within the executive branch, with varying degrees of independence from the president.) The EPA, for instance, has wide latitude in identifying and restricting pollutants, because Congress does not want to legislate every new regulation. Instead, it gives the EPA certain guidelines, then leaves it to the agency's scientists to determine what rules would best serve the public. The Clean Air Act does not detail every jot and tittle of power plant regulations; the act merely compels these plants to use "the best system of emission reduction" using current technology and asks the EPA to decide if plants have met that standard. That delegation would probably fail Gorsuch's test.

There are countless more examples. Some agencies—such as the Federal Communications Commission, which regulates radio, TV, wire, satellite, and cable—are directed to act in the "public interest." Others such as the Federal Trade Commission, which promotes consumer protection and antitrust. are told to punish "deceptive" conduct—without a precise definition of deception. To Gorsuch, such commands may be unlawfully broad.

Skepticism toward federal agencies is not entirely unwarranted; they may sometimes blunder. Luckily, there are numerous checks and balances built into the system, most importantly the ability of Congress to alter an agency decision through legislation. Congress can overturn or supplant agency rules; it retains all "legislative powers" under the U.S. Constitution. Gorsuch believes that excess delegation of this power violates the Constitution. But as University of Michigan law professor Nicholas Bagley noted in a *New York Times* opinion piece titled "'Most of Government Is Unconstitutional': Did the Supreme Court Just Suggest That It Is Prepared to Agree with That Statement?," the Constitution also empowers Congress "to make all Laws which shall be necessary and proper for carrying into Execution" its authorities.

"Congress does not *surrender* its legislative power by delegating," Bagley wrote. "It *exercises* that power."

Gorsuch, Roberts, and Thomas disagree. So too, it seems, does Alito. His compact concurrence may be a clue as to why *Gundy* took 261 days to decide. Since Alito is willing to "reconsider" the court's nondelegation doctrine, he may have originally voted with the conservatives in *Gundy*. The court tries to work around 4–4 splits, which render the case a regrettable waste of time. It may be that Alito eventually relented, casting a fifth vote to affirm Gundy's conviction without joining Kagan's opinion. By doing so, Alito gave Gorsuch an opportunity to write his dissent preparing a frontal assault on the administrative state.

Whatever the motivation behind his vote in *Gundy*, Alito won't have to wait much longer for a majority of the court to reevaluate the nondelegation doctrine. While serving on the court of appeals, Kavanaugh routinely voted to limit agency power; the White House boasted that he "overruled federal agency action 75 times." He consistently voted to invalidate EPA regulations, espousing a strictly circumscribed role for agencies. And he criticized the administrative state as "a headless fourth branch of the U.S. Government" that poses "a significant threat to individual liberty and to the constitutional system of separation of powers."

In other words, Kavanaugh seems poised to join the conservative justices in striking down federal laws that, in their view, give agencies too much power. His predecessor, Justice Anthony Kennedy, was more moderate on the matter and forestalled the sea change that Gorsuch eagerly awaits. With Kavanaugh sitting in Kennedy's seat, there may be nothing to hold the court back from declaring, in Kagan's words, that "most of Government is unconstitutional."

Four days after *Gundy* came down, the court released another ruling pertaining to the powers of the administrative state in *Kisor v. Wilkie*. It was, put simply, a shocker. Few if any court watchers correctly predicted the outcome in *Kisor*. The case was expected to be a conservative rout. Instead, as she had in *Gundy*, Kagan finagled a solution that kept the law more or less stable. Against all odds, she held the line.

Kisor involved a Vietnam War veteran, James Kisor, who sought disability benefits from the Department of Veterans Affairs (VA). Kisor believes that he developed post-traumatic stress disorder (PTSD) after participating in an action called Operation Harvest Moon. In 1982 a psychiatrist found that he did *not* have PTSD, so the VA denied his claim. Kisor reopened his claim in 2006 after a psychiatrist found that he *did* have PTSD. This time, the VA granted his claim but denied him retroactive benefits. A VA regulation allows retroactive benefits only when a service member provides "relevant" records that were not initially considered. Kisor sued, insisting that he had put forth new service records that confirmed his participation in Operation Harvest Moon. But were these really "relevant" to the denial of his claim in 1982? After all, the VA first turned him down because it thought he had no PTSD, *not* because it thought he hadn't fought in Operation Harvest Moon.

To resolve this dispute, the U.S. Court of Appeals for the Federal Circuit deferred to the VA's interpretation of the regulation. According to the VA, a record is "relevant" if it "counter[s] the basis of the prior denial." Kisor's new records did not counter the basis of his 1982 denial because he had not proved that he had PTSD back then. So, the Federal Circuit sided with the VA.

This approach to agency regulations is called *Auer* deference. It is named after a unanimous 1997 decision written by Justice Antonin Scalia in *Auer v. Robbins*, which held that courts must defer to an agency's "reasonable interpretation" of its own ambiguous regulations. And it is almost universally despised by conservative academics and jurists. Multiple Supreme Court justices, including Scalia himself, have disavowed *Auer* deference. This approach, Scalia wrote in 2013, "has no principled basis but contravenes one of the great rules of separation of powers: He who writes a law must not adjudge its violation." (Scalia never publicly explained his change of heart.)

Every conservative on the court today has questioned *Auer* deference, and Roberts invited a challenge to the rule in a 2013 concurrence. When Kisor appealed his case to the Supreme Court, he accepted Roberts's invitation and asked the justices to overturn *Auer*. In taking the case, the court agreed to decide just one question: whether *Auer* should be overturned. During oral arguments, the goose seemed cooked; Roberts, Alito, Gorsuch, and Kavanaugh took turns trashing *Auer* from every angle. (As usual, Thomas did not speak.) They left Justice Stephen Breyer to bemoan that the court was preparing for a "judicial power grab."

Then on the morning of June 24, Roberts announced that the court had a decision in *Kisor v. Wilkie*—and that it would be read by Justice Kagan. *Justice Kagan?* As she began reading her opinion, it became clear that the court had spared *Auer*. Specifically, Roberts had joined with the four liberal justices to uphold the doctrine, over the outraged dissent of the remaining conservatives. How did she do it?

By mounting a vigorous defense of *Auer*, then narrowing it to a nub that Roberts could live with, Kagan's masterful opinion took pains to illustrate the myriad cases in which *Auer* deference plays a useful role. Some are prosaic: Does a "jar of truffle pâté" qualify as a liquid or gel subject to Transportation Security Administration (TSA) regulations? Others are arcane: Does the Food and Drug Administration (FDA) give exclusive rights to a drug manufacturer who "created a new 'active moiety' by joining a previously approved moiety to lysine through a non-ester covalent bond?"

"If you are a judge," Kagan noted, "you probably have no idea of what the FDA's rule means" or how to resolve a clash of the moieties. And that's okay. Congress is "attuned to the comparative advantages of agencies over courts in making such policy judgments." Unlike courts, agencies "can conduct factual investigations, can consult with affected parties, can consider how their experts have handled similar issues over the long course of administering a regulatory program." Consider "our TSA example," Kagan wrote:

> In most of their applications, terms like "liquids" and "gels" are clear enough. (Traveler checklist: Pretzels OK; water not.) But resolving the uncertain issues—the truffle pâtés or olive tapenades of the world—requires getting in the weeds of the rule's policy: Why does TSA ban liquids and gels in the first instance? What makes them dangerous? Can a potential hijacker use pâté jars in the same way as soda cans?

Congress entrusted the TSA to create rules for safe air travel, then interpret those rules in light of the agency's mission. Courts should respect agencies' "unique expertise" when "new issues demanding new policy calls" arise. Thus, when a rule is ambiguous and an agency's interpretation is reasonable, courts should defer to the agency.

At the same time that Kagain praised *Auer*, she took "the opportunity to restate" its reach. Deference only applies when a regulation "is genuinely ambiguous," meaning a court can find "no single right answer" after exhausting "all the 'traditional tools' of construction." Moreover, the agency's interpretation must be "reasonable," meaning "it must come within the zone of ambiguity the court has identified after employing all its interpretive tools." Finally, to receive *Auer* deference, an agency interpretation must be its "official position," must implicate the agency's "substantive expertise," and must reflect "fair and considered judgment."

If an agency can check all these boxes, it will receive *Auer* deference. If not, courts are on their own. Kagan wrapped up her opinion by sending *Kisor* back down to the Federal Circuit to determine whether the VA regulation is "genuinely ambiguous" and whether the VA's position "reflects the considered judgment of the agency as a whole."

Kagan's opinion was obviously a compromise to draw Roberts's vote. That it worked is no surprise. Since joining the court, Kagan has presented herself as a moderating voice of reason. She has operated as a kind of shadow chief who shares Roberts's institutional concerns, his desire for consensus and judicial humility, while viewing the law through a more progressive lens. Her opinions are careful and modest, reflecting deep respect for precedent. She forgoes indignation and ornate rhetoric, favoring direct, highly readable prose. If any justice can unite warring wings of the court, it is Kagan. She will not sacrifice her principles, but she will make concessions to build coalitions that will anchor the law in sensible, centrist jurisprudence. And that is exactly what she did in *Kisor*.

In dissent, Gorsuch accused the majority of placing "new and nebulous qualifications and limitations on *Auer*" to keep it "on life support." The doctrine, he wrote, "emerges maimed and enfeebled—in truth, zombified." He called on the court to "stop this business of making up excuses for judges to abdicate their job of interpreting the law." Gorsuch's sprawling opinion provided constitutional, statutory, and policy reasons for overturning *Auer*, dwelling on its role in "the explosive growth of the administrative state over the last half-century." But he concluded that Kagan left *Auer* "so riddled with holes" that it barely retained any force.

"I hope that our judicial colleagues on other courts will take courage from today's ruling," Gorsuch proclaimed, "and realize that it has transformed *Auer* into a paper tiger."

Thomas, Alito, and Kavanaugh joined the bulk of Gorsuch's dissent. Both Roberts (who joined the important parts of Kagan's ruling) and Kavanaugh (who dissented) wrote short opinions to make two points. First, both believed that there was not much "distance between the majority and [the dissent]," because Kagan had severely constrained *Auer* deference. Second, both pointed out that the decision did not "touch upon" a related doctrine, *Chevron* deference.

Here, the two justices implicitly acknowledged that *Kisor v. Wilkie* is really just a preview for a bigger battle: the fight over *Chevron* deference. Under this doctrine, which was devised in 1984, courts must defer to an agency's reasonable interpretation of *federal law*. If a statute is foggy, an agency can make its own decision about how best to enforce it. And so long as that decision is not unreasonable, the courts must uphold it.

To conservatives such as *National Review*'s David French, "*Chevron* is the Great Satan. *Auer* is the Little Satan." It is *Chevron*, these critics claim, that has allowed the administrative state to snowball in size and intrude in every American's life. It is *Chevron* that has prevented courts from compelling agencies to follow the letter of the law, allowing bureaucrats to shoehorn their policy preferences into inapt statutes. It is *Chevron* that animates the "headless fourth branch," which drains Congress of its vitality and centralizes power in an unaccountable bureaucracy. For conservatives, *Chevron* deference and constitutional governance cannot coexist.

It is also *Chevron* that allows the government to do the everyday work of executing the law. Without it, agencies would often be incapable of responding to the changing needs of a large and diverse nation through creative but lawful interpretations of existing statutes. Killing *Chevron* would also transfer power from the executive branch to the courts, giving judges the ultimate authority to interpret ambiguous laws. Agencies are not directly accountable to the people, but most are accountable to the president— and when the people do not like the executive branch's actions, they can vote the president out. Federal courts are accountable to virtually no one. The people cannot replace federal judges at the ballot box.

Gundy and *Kisor* suggest that four and perhaps five justices are ready to scrap *Chevron* and commence a slash-and-burn approach to federal statutes and agency rules. If their goal is to decrease the size of government by any means necessary, they will succeed. But a smaller government is not always a more competent one. For all that Americans complain about bureaucracy, they may come to miss the administrative state when it is gone.

Democracy Imperiled

The Gerrymandering Case

When drawing North Carolina's current congressional districts, Republican lawmakers had one overriding goal: to elect as many Republicans as possible. We know this because they told us. Representative David Lewis, who led the redistricting process, announced: "I think electing Republicans is better than electing Democrats. So I drew this map to help foster what I think is better for the country." He explained that his map had created seats for ten Republicans and three Democrats because he did not think it was "possible to draw a map with 11 Republicans and 2 Democrats." Lewis's map worked exactly as planned. The next election cycle, Republicans won just 53 percent of the statewide vote—but took ten of North Carolina's thirteen congressional districts.

Lewis had been brazen for a reason. In 2016 a federal court invalidated the state's existing map because districts had been drawn along racial lines, forcing Republicans to devise a new map. As Lewis knew, the U.S. Supreme Court has long held that such *racial* gerrymandering violates the U.S. Constitution. Yet the justices had never struck down a *partisan* gerrymander or agreed on a standard to gauge their legality. The court's inaction convinced politicians such as Lewis that they could gerrymander the opposing party out of power so long as they relied on political affiliation, not race, to draw maps. Lewis boasted about his partisan gerrymander because he wanted to show the public and the courts that he had not broken the law. His map might be ugly and unfair—but, he insisted, it was not illegal.

At the time, Lewis was making a dicey bet. Five justices on the Supreme Court had a clear interest in placing constitutional limits on political redistricting. Justice Anthony Kennedy, the crucial swing vote, wrote in 2004's *Vieth v. Jubelirer* that "excessive" partisan gerrymandering imposed an unconstitutional burden on voters' "representational rights." Still, he declined to intervene until he could identify "suitable standards for measuring this burden." Once the courts had devised a "workable standard," Kennedy would be willing to strike down partisan gerrymanders that go too far.

Kennedy's *Vieth* opinion set off a fifteen-year scramble among academics and advocates to locate a standard that would satisfy the justice. In the meantime, partisan gerrymanders grew more potent. North Carolina is a perfect example. Using sophisticated technology, political operatives drew contorted districts that "packed" most Democrats into a few deep-blue districts and then "cracked" the rest throughout safe Republican districts. Mapmakers' lines cut through counties, cities, and neighborhoods. Several ingenious districts snaked around country clubs, relying on Republican inhabitants of the surrounding communities to cancel out Democratic votes elsewhere. These "packed and cracked" districts made no geographic sense; they did not represent any community or political subdivision. Their sole purpose was to rig elections.

As North Carolina voters watched Republicans entrench their power through partisan gerrymandering, voting rights experts proposed an array of standards that Kennedy could use to rein in the practice. Progressive advocates seized upon their work to challenge the North Carolina map as unconstitutional. By the time their case, *Rucho v. Common Cause*, reached the Supreme Court, though, Kennedy was gone, replaced by Justice Brett Kavanaugh. After just a few months on the bench, the newest justice held the fate of partisan gerrymandering in his hands.

Drawing districts to boost the power of the ruling party and dilute votes for the opposition is as old as the American republic. The word "gerrymander" was coined when, in 1812, Massachusetts governor Elbridge Gerry approved a district so twisted that critics compared it to a salamander. "Gerrymandering" occurs in the creation of both legislative districts (which make up state legislatures) and congressional districts (which make up the House of Representatives). For most of the nation's history, gerrymandering was used in extreme malapportionment—the creation of electoral districts with unequal ratios of voters to representatives.

In his definitive study of malapportionment *On Democracy's Doorstep*, J. Douglas Smith laid out the appalling inequality of legislative maps in 1960. That year, Vermont had house districts with as few as 38 people and as many as 33,000. The population of New Jersey's senate districts ranged from 48,555 people to 923,545. Georgia's senate districts ranged in population from 13,050 to 556,326, Idaho's from 915 to 93,460, Arizona's from 3,868 to 331,755, and California's from 14,294 to 6 *million*.

State senators elected from each district, of course, had equal votes in the legislature. The malapportionment of their districts, however, meant that votes cast by residents of one part of the state were vastly more powerful than votes cast by resident in another region. In Vermont, for example, if you lived in the state's smallest house district in 1960, your vote counted about 868 times more than a resident of the largest house district. The power of your vote depended on your geographic location.

This style of gerrymandering was crude but effective. In much of the country, lawmakers feared the growing political clout of urban Americans. The nation's booming cities were filled with immigrants, Jews, Catholics, and racial minorities who seemed poised to seize control of state governance and pass progressive reforms. Legislatures responded by cramming (diverse) city dwellers in a few massive districts, then giving (mostly white) rural residents far more representatives per capita. Racism and nativism undoubtedly motivated twentieth-century malappointment, but the chief goal was partisan. The conservative party—Republicans in the North and Democrats in the South—entrenched their own power by drawing gerrymandered legislative districts that diluted votes for their opponents.

Because state legislatures have historically drawn congressional as well as legislative districts, gerrymandering warped the House of Representatives too. In 1960, state legislators had concocted absurdly malapportioned congressional districts that made a mockery of the nickname "the People's House." According to Smith's study, in nineteen states the largest House district had more than twice the number of residents as the smallest. In Texas, the largest district was four times more populous than the smallest. In Michigan, that ratio exceeded seven to one. The state's House districts ranged in population from 117,431 to 802,994 people.

This injustice was in part the fault of the Supreme Court. In 1946's *Colegrove v. Green*, the Supreme Court ruled 4–3 that federal courts could not address malapportionment—over a biting dissent by the liberal justices. (One justice had just died and another had taken leave, leaving a seven-member court.) Justice Felix Frankfurter's plurality opinion held that gerrymandering constitutes a question "of a peculiarly political nature, and therefore not [suitable] for judicial determination." Out of "due regard for the effective working of our Government," Frankfurter wrote, the court "ought not to enter this political thicket." Rather, the "remedy for unfairness in districting is to secure State legislatures that will apportion properly, or to invoke the ample powers of Congress."

Frankfurter did not seem to recognize the contradiction in his claim. How could victims of malapportionment "secure State legislatures" when legislatures had drawn districts to lock these victims out of power? It is true that under the Constitution, Congress may compel states to draw fair congressional districts. But myriad members of the House owed their seats to malapportionment. Did Frankfurter really believe that a gerrymandered House would vote to stop congressional gerrymandering?

As the statistics from 1960 illustrate, malapportionment grew more radical after *Colegrove*. Frankfurter's prediction that the people might end gerrymandering through the democratic process was proved wrong. But by that point, the Supreme Court had moved to the left under the leadership of Chief Justice Earl Warren. And in 1962 Warren and his colleagues overturned *Colegrove* in *Baker v. Carr*, ruling that federal courts had sufficient "competence" to address malapportionment (Frankfurter dissented). The court had already struck down electoral boundaries drawn on the basis of race and was no longer reluctant to assess other forms of gerrymandering. Warren would describe *Baker* as "the most vital decision" of his tenure.

The dominoes fell quickly after *Baker*. In 1963's *Gray v. Sanders*, the Supreme Court announced the principle of "one person, one vote." In 1964's *Wesberry v. Sanders*, the court held that the Constitution requires states to draw congressional districts of roughly equal population so that representatives are chosen "by the People." That same year in *Reynolds v. Sims*, the court ruled that state house and senate districts must also be equal in population "as nearly as is practicable" to comply with the equal protection clause. (The court later clarified that the population could not deviate by more than 10 percent across districts.) The court's "reapportionment revolution" obliged most states to redraw both legislative and congressional districts within several years.

But the revolution did not end gerrymandering. Instead, lawmakers adapted to "one person, one vote" by drawing districts of equal population along racial and partisan lines. The Supreme Court restricted racial gerrymandering under the equal protection clause and the Voting Rights Act of 1964, curbing states' ability to dilute minority votes. However, the court was not nearly as vigilant in policing partisan gerrymanders. In 1986's *Davis v. Bandemer*, a majority of the justices agreed that partisan gerrymandering can violate the equal protection clause and that challenges to political redistricting are "justiciable" (meaning federal courts can address them). Yet the justices splintered on the proper standard, leaving lower courts with little guidance to determine when these gerrymanders crossed the constitutional line.

Eighteen years later in *Vieth*, a four-justice plurality tried but failed to overturn *Bandemer* and hold that partisan gerrymandering claims constitute a nonjusticiable "political question." That is when Kennedy issued his puzzling opinion declaring that such claims are not justiciable *yet* but might be once the court found a better standard for measuring them. Kennedy also shifted the jurisprudential basis of these claims, explaining that partisan gerrymandering infringes upon voters' First Amendment right to participate in the electoral process and associate with a political party. "First Amendment concerns arise," Kennedy wrote, "where an apportionment has the purpose and effect of burdening a group of voters' representational rights."

Kennedy's plea for "judicially manageable standards" produced results fast. Two tests, partisan symmetry and the efficiency gap, became especially popular. Designed by scholars, these tests use mathematical formulas to measure the scale of a gerrymander. They identify maps that entrench the majority party's power so effectively that it cannot realistically lose its stranglehold on the legislature. As a result, supporters of the opposite party cannot achieve representation, even when they win a majority of the vote.

Voting rights advocates deployed these tests in a lawsuit against Wisconsin's legislative map. In 2012, Republicans won 48.6 percent of the statewide vote—and sixty out of ninety-nine seats in the state assembly. In 2014, they received 52 percent of the vote and won sixty-three seats. In 2016, they received the same percentage of the statewide vote, and their majority crept up to sixty-four seats. These results set off alarm bells under both the partisan symmetry and efficiency gap standards. Democratic voters accused mapmakers of violating their constitutional rights.

A federal district court agreed in 2016, relying in part on the partisan symmetry and efficiency gap tests to find that Wisconsin's gerrymander crossed a constitutional boundary. Due to a quirk in federal law, the Supreme Court *had* to hear *Gill v. Whitford*. While the court generally gets to decide which cases to take, it has "mandatory jurisdiction" over gerrymandering cases, meaning it *must* hear these appeals. So, in October 2017 the court heard arguments in *Gill* and appeared hopelessly confused. At one point, Chief Justice John Roberts dismissed both partisan symmetry and the efficiency gap as "sociological gobbledygook."

After oral arguments in *Gill* the court took up another partisan gerrymandering case, *Benisek v. Lamone. Benisek* was a challenge to Maryland's Sixth Congressional District; a Democratic gerrymander joined the state's conservative panhandle to its liberal suburbs near the District of Columbia. Republican voters argued that their votes had been diluted in retaliation for their political views, a violation of the First Amendment. A federal district court rejected their claims. And at arguments in March 2018, the Supreme Court appeared skeptical of this "retaliation" theory.

Both *Gill* and *Benisek* ended with a whimper in June 2018. The court unanimously punted on *Gill* in a decision by Roberts, who wrote that the plaintiffs had not established "standing" (i.e., a "constitutional injury" that courts can address). Justice Elena Kagan wrote a concurrence laying out the case that partisan gerrymandering "degrad[es] the nation's democracy" by infringing on voters' "First Amendment right of association." The other liberal justices joined her opinion, but Kennedy did not. Fourteen years after his *Vieth* concurrence, Kennedy was still not prepared to rein in partisan gerrymandering. The court also punted on *Benisek*. Nine days later, Kennedy announced his retirement.

Thanks to mandatory jurisdiction, the justices' punts did not last long. Judges began invalidating partisan gerrymanders left and right, striking down maps in North Carolina, Ohio, and Michigan. These rulings seethe with indignation over lawmakers' effort to rig elections for their own party. They describe gerrymandering as "repugnant to representative democracy," a "noxious" and "pernicious practice that undermines our democracy" and "violates the core purpose of legislative apportionment." It was as if lower court judges, both Republican and Democratic appointees, were lobbying the Supreme Court to stand up for voting rights.

In March 2019, the Supreme Court heard two of these cases: *Rucho*, from North Carolina, and *Benisek*, from Maryland. (After the 2018 punt in *Benisek*, a federal court threw out Maryland's Sixth Congressional District, and the case boomeranged right back to the Supreme Court.) This time around, all eyes were on Kavanaugh. Roberts had shown his hand the previous year with his widely scorned "sociological gobbledygook" gibe. (The president of the American Sociological Association even sent the chief justice an open letter chastising his "lack of understanding of social science.") Justices Clarence Thomas, Neil Gorsuch, and Samuel Alito had already scorned the notion of courts stepping in to fix partisan maps.

At oral arguments Kavanaugh—like Kennedy before him—appeared genuinely torn. When Maryland solicitor general Steven M. Sullivan approached the lectern to defend his own state's gerrymander, though, Kavanaugh grew notably more engaged. As Sullivan asserted that the shape of Maryland's Sixth District was not "heavily influenced" by "partisan politics," Kavanaugh looked incredulous.

"The stated goal was 7–1," he told Sullivan—meaning Democratic politicians declared that they wanted to create seven Democratic districts (including the sixth) and just one Republican district. "I don't think you should run away from the obvious." Kavanaugh then ran through the geographic absurdity of the map with surprising specificity—"You've got Easton grouped with Carroll County!" A Maryland resident, Kavanaugh seemed to recognize the harms of the state's Democratic gerrymander. But he also asked a few ambivalent questions suggesting that he thought the plaintiffs were demanding "proportional representation," a system in which parties win seats in rough proportion to the votes cast for them.

In June the court issued its decision in the two disputes, consolidating them into a single decision, *Rucho*. It was a crushing defeat for the plaintiffs. Kavanaugh had done what his predecessor, Kennedy, would not: voted to expel partisan gerrymandering claims from federal court—forever.

By a 5–4 vote, the court ruled that these claims present a nonjusticiable "political question." Roberts's majority opinion was predictably dismissive of the proposed analytical frameworks for measuring extreme redistricting. "Partisan gerrymandering claims," he alleged, "invariably [express] a desire for proportional representation," which is not required by the Constitution. They ask federal courts "to apportion political power as a matter of fairness," a task that courts are not "authorized to do."

"There are no legal standards discernible in the Constitution for making such judgments," Roberts wrote, "let alone limited and precise standards that are clear, manageable, and politically neutral." He added that none of the "'tests' for evaluating partisan gerrymandering claims . . . provides a solid grounding for judges to take the extraordinary step of reallocating power and influence between political parties." Because he could not identify an appropriate standard, Roberts slammed the federal courthouse doors shut to partisan gerrymandering plaintiffs.

In a dissent joined by the other liberals, Kagan accused the chief justice of abdicating his judicial duty. "For the first time ever," she began, "this Court refuses to remedy a constitutional violation because it thinks the task beyond judicial capabilities. And not just any constitutional violation." Kagan continued:

> The partisan gerrymanders in these cases deprived citizens of the most fundamental of their constitutional rights: the rights to participate equally in the political process, to join with others to advance political beliefs, and to choose their political representatives. In so doing, the partisan gerrymanders here debased

and dishonored our democracy, turning upside-down the core American idea that all governmental power derives from the people. These gerrymanders enabled politicians to entrench themselves in office as against voters' preferences. They promoted partisanship above respect for the popular will. They encouraged a politics of polarization and dysfunction. If left unchecked, gerrymanders like the ones here may irreparably damage our system of government.

Today, Kagan wrote, mapmakers "have access to more granular data about party preference and voting behavior than ever before," and "advancements in computing technology have enabled mapmakers to put that information to use with unprecedented efficiency and precision." Look at Pennsylvania, where Democrats won 51 percent of the statewide vote but seized just five of eighteen House seats under a Republican gerrymander; Ohio, where Democrats won 47 percent of the statewide vote but never took more than four of sixteen House seats; or North Carolina and Maryland, where lawmakers provided *smoking-gun evidence* that their flagrant and effective gerrymanders were intended to rig elections in their favor.

"Is that how American democracy is supposed to work?" Kagan asked. "I have yet to meet the person who thinks so."

And we have not hit rock bottom. Gerrymandering will only get worse as data "becomes ever more fine-grained and data analysis techniques continue to improve." This willful dilution of votes, Kagan insisted, infringes on equal protection as well as freedom of speech and association. Indeed, the majority did not seriously contest the existence of a constitutional violation implicit in partisan gerrymandering. The majority merely held that it could not find a workable legal standard.

To Kagan, the majority's decision to give up on a standard is nonsensical. "What it says can't be done," she wrote, "*has* been done." The lower courts developed a test that the Supreme Court could easily adopt. Did the majority party intend to dilute votes to entrench its own power? Did it succeed? If so, the map is presumptively unlawful unless the state can provide some "legitimate, non-partisan justification" for its bias. Without this justification, the map must go.

This test does not mandate "proportional representation." It identifies and eradicates "the extreme manipulation of district lines for partisan gain." And identifying unconstitutionally "extreme" maps is not difficult. Kagan explained that plaintiffs can offer a "boatload of alternative districting plans" to show that the state's map was not just an outlier but was also an "out-out-out-outlier." In North Carolina, for instance, an expert produced 3,000 maps using traditional nonpartisan redistricting criteria. *Every single map* produced at least one more Democratic congressional district than the state's map. "How much is too much?" Kagan asked. "This much is too much." And yet the majority upheld North Carolina's map as well as Maryland's—preventing all victims of partisan gerrymandering from pursuing their claims in federal court.

Kagan ended on a note of despondency:

> Of all times to abandon the Court's duty to declare the law, this was not the one. The practices challenged in these cases imperil our system of government. Part of

the Court's role in that system is to defend its foundations. None is more important than free and fair elections. With respect but deep sadness, I dissent.

Rucho is a hugely consequential decision. The ruling
ensures that lawmakers in a majority of states will continue to manipulate district lines to dilute votes for the
opposite party. Worse, lawmakers can now redistrict along
political lines without fear of federal courts halting their
efforts. By giving them a free pass, the Supreme Court may
have exacerbated the problem.

The majority asserted that citizens did not "condemn
complaints about districting to echo into a void." Citizens,
Roberts wrote, can pursue other solutions to partisan
gerrymandering, such as independent redistricting commissions. This suggestion is ironic, because the court only
upheld such bodies by a 5–4 vote in 2015's *Arizona State
Legislature v. Arizona Independent Redistricting Commission.* (Kennedy voted with the liberals to save independent
redistricting.) The dissenting conservative justices, led by
Roberts, protested that only state legislatures held the
power to draw districts under the Constitution. In *Rucho*,
then, the chief justice advised citizens to adopt a reform
that he decried as unconstitutional just four years earlier.

Even if the post-Kennedy court upheld independent
redistricting commissions, however, they are not viable in
most of the country. So far these commissions have been
adopted via ballot initiative—but a majority of states do not
allow citizens to put reforms to a direct vote. Instead, citizens
must go through the legislature, and history proves that legislators will not willingly give up their power to gerrymander. And even when voters *do* pass reforms, the legislature

can claw them back. In Missouri, residents overwhelmingly approved a proposal that turned over legislative redistricting to a state demographer in 2018. Lawmakers are already in the process of eliminating that reform.

Roberts pointed to another avenue of relief: state courts, which can interpret their own state constitutions to limit partisan gerrymandering. Forty-nine state constitutions protect the right to vote, and a majority guarantee that elections shall be "free and equal" or "free and open." Because state supreme courts are the final arbiters of state law, they can use these provisions to invalidate gerrymandered maps. The Pennsylvania Supreme Court did just that in 2018, ruling that a gerrymandered congressional map ran afoul of the state constitution's free and equal elections clause. The court commissioned a new nonpartisan map that produced vastly more competitive elections. In 2016 under the Republican gerrymander, Republicans won thirteen of eighteen House seats. In 2018 under the new map, Republicans and Democrats each won nine seats.

Certainly, state supreme courts deserve credit for curtailing partisan gerrymandering. But it is curious to hear Roberts crediting them, since these courts debunk his central claim. The chief justice believes that federal courts cannot competently police partisan gerrymandering, but state courts have done exactly that—to great success. Some, such as Pennsylvania's, have operated under state constitutions that are no more precise than the U.S. Constitution on the matter of redistricting. As Kagan wondered in her dissent, "what do those courts know that this Court does not? If they can develop and apply neutral and manageable standards to identify unconstitutional gerrymanders, why couldn't we?"

To express her frustration with the majority, Kagan read her dissent from the bench. Several weeks later, speaking at Georgetown University Law School, she decried the decision as "abysmally wrong" and declared that there is "no part of me that's ever going to [accept it]." There is no middle ground between her dissent and Roberts's majority opinion. They reflect irreconcilable philosophical differences between the two justices—and, by extension, the two wings of the court. The conservatives wanted to wash their hands clean of partisan gerrymandering, to keep the federal judiciary out of these heated, unpleasant disputes. The liberals saw an egregious constitutional violation that they are duty-bound to redress. The majority is not especially worried that manipulating district lines will have corrosive effects on self-governance. The dissenters believe that nothing less than democracy is at stake.

History, in other words, is repeating itself. Roberts had filled Frankfurter's shoes in *Colegrove*, attempting to keep his court out of the "political thicket." Kagan revived the objections of *Colegrove*'s dissenters, who believed that the court had a responsibility to safeguard "the right to vote and to have that vote effectively counted." *Colegrove*'s dissenters eventually won the day in *Baker v. Carr*. It is too soon to tell if *Rucho*'s dissenters will similarly see their opinion become law.

In *Rucho*, Kagan acted as the conscience of the court. She appealed to readers directly, twice exhorting them to ask if this is "how American democracy is supposed to work." Her opinion, eloquent but straightforward and engaging, speaks not just to the majority but also to the country and to future justices. As Kagan explained at the Georgetown event,

I didn't really pull [any] punches about the importance that I thought that decision had about our political system and the way we govern ourselves. . . . There, you're not writing the dissent because you just thought you saw the thing differently and you think everybody should know that there were two sides to this issue. You are writing the dissent because you want to convince the future. You want to convince the present, too. But for all those people out there who, in some way, can carry on the efforts against this kind of undermining of democracy—go for it.

Here once again, Kagan embraced her role as the shadow chief justice. Unable to build compromise with Roberts, she attacked his reasoning from every angle. She looked ahead to a future when a majority of the court agreed with her jurisprudence. And she laid the groundwork for that future court to enshrine her own ideas into the law. Roberts may have gathered five votes for his position in *Rucho*, but Kagan intends to win the battle of ideas.

There is one final detail in *Rucho* worth mentioning. North Carolina's gerrymandered maps—as well as Pennsylvania's, Wisconsin's, and those in other swing states—were the result of Project REDMAP, a well-funded initiative of the Republican State Leadership Committee. Project RED-MAP began in 2009, when Republicans realized that they could control the redistricting process if they seized statehouses in 2010. (Districts are redrawn at the start of each decade using new census data.) They succeeded, flipping nineteen legislative bodies that year. Project REDMAP lent Republican lawmakers high-tech software and skilled operatives to draw durable gerrymanders that would preserve Republican control for the next decade.

Some of the nation's most notorious gerrymanders, including North Carolina's, were drawn by one man: Thomas Hofeller, a key player in Project REDMAP. Hofeller was a lifelong Republican operative who pioneered modern gerrymandering, helping Republicans throughout the country entrench their power through redistricting. When the justices reviewed Hofeller's work in *Rucho*, they had no idea that he would play a major role in the final and most explosive decision of the term: the census case.

Drawing the Line on Lies

The Census Case

No recent U.S. Supreme Court case involves more intrigue and deception than *Department of Commerce v. New York*. Arguably O.T. 2018's biggest blockbuster, *Department of Commerce* turned on a matter of immense importance: whether Donald Trump's administration can add a citizenship question to the 2020 census. The Census Bureau itself found that asking individuals about their citizenship status would diminish the quality of the survey, decreasing electoral representation for immigrants and Hispanics. Ample evidence also demonstrates that officials misrepresented their reason for seeking citizenship data. The Supreme Court therefore had to decide whether the administration could legally warp the census *and* lie about its justification for doing so.

Then after oral arguments in *Department of Commerce*, the plaintiffs dropped a bombshell: they had uncovered further proof that the true purpose of the citizenship question was to favor white Republican voters. This evidence was buried in a trove of materials left behind by Thomas Hofeller, the Republican Party gerrymandering guru, who died in 2018. His estranged daughter had turned over his files to voting rights advocates, who realized that Trump's Department of Justice (DOJ) had relied on Hofeller's work to devise its pretense for the citizenship question. *Department of Commerce* began to resemble a soap opera.

The Supreme Court did not put an end to this drama when it released its ruling in June. Chief Justice John Roberts sided with the conservatives on almost every point and then veered left at the very end of his opinion, delivering an ambiguous victory to the plaintiffs. His confusing decision set off an astonishing chain of events as the president fought to keep the citizenship question alive, even as administration attorneys told the courts that it was dead. In the end Trump gave up, bowing to the inevitable. Although the chief justice had theoretically allowed the administration to revive the citizenship question, he left no real room for Trump to maneuver it back onto the census.

Roberts's vote does not augur a broader shift to the left. His opinion was not liberal but instead was deeply institutionalist, preserving the court's legitimacy and independence. The chief justice refused to shut his eyes to the overwhelming evidence of bad faith and deceit that administration officials deployed to defend the citizenship question. And he reminded the president that while he remains a conservative jurist, he is not willing to humiliate himself or his court at the behest of the Trump administration.

To understand Roberts's split decision in *Department of Commerce*, it is important to see how the administration bungled a fight it probably could have won. That fight began shortly after Wilbur Ross became secretary of commerce in February 2017.

The Senate confirmed Ross, a wealthy businessman, by a vote of 72–27. His control over the 2020 census was not a topic of interest during his hearings, perhaps because Democrats did not anticipate his involvement in the process. But the Census Bureau is located within the Department of Commerce, and the secretary has extensive authority over its operations.

Upon taking office, Ross focused on one idea in particular: adding a citizenship question to the decennial census—the survey that every resident of the country must fill out each decade. There has not been such a question on the decennial census since 1950; instead, the bureau includes it on the American Community Survey, a yearly survey distributed to about one in thirty-six households. Ross intended to bring the citizenship question back to the decennial census for the first time in seventy years.

Early in his tenure Ross spoke about the citizenship question with Kris Kobach, then the Kansas secretary of state. Kobach had gained notoriety for championing laws that required voters to prove their citizenship status, contending that thousands of noncitizens had voted in Kansas. (He was unable to corroborate this claim in court.) Kobach urged Ross to add a citizenship question, asserting that it would be an "essential" tool to resolve "the problem" of counting noncitizens for congressional redistricting.

There is in fact no such problem. The U.S. Constitution states that representatives must be apportioned "among the several States according to their respective numbers, counting the whole number of persons in each State." In addition, the Constitution requires the "actual enumeration," speaks of "persons" not "citizens," and requires congressional districts to be drawn using this data. Nevertheless, Ross agreed with Kobach and embarked on a quest to add the citizenship question. Ross also made the issue a top priority for his staff.

The Constitution gives Congress power over the census. But Congress has delegated much of its authority to the secretary of commerce, including the ability to add new questions. In modifying the census, the secretary must comply with the Administrative Procedure Act (APA). Among other things, the APA requires that his actions not be "arbitrary and capricious." Ross knew that he had to concoct a rationale for the citizenship question that would satisfy this standard. Ideally, he decided, he would persuade a *different* agency to ask him to include the question. That way, its inclusion would appear practical and advantageous, not random or dubious.

Ross reached out to officials at the Department of Homeland Security to ask if they would formally request a citizenship question. They declined. He reached out to officials at the DOJ's Executive Office for Immigration Review with the same entreaty. They too declined. Frustrated, Ross pulled rank on DOJ attorneys, threatening to call the attorney general if they would not request a citizenship question. Eventually Attorney General Jeff Sessions did intervene. Sessions overruled lower-ranked officials and asked John Gore, then Acting Assistant Attorney General for the Civil Rights Division, to work with the Commerce Department to create a justification.

Gore collaborated with Mark Neuman, Ross's adviser, to develop the Voting Rights Act (VRA) rationale. Neuman wrote a draft letter laying out this theory; Gore adapted the letter and gave it to Arthur Gary, general counsel of the DOJ's Justice Management Division, to sign. Because Gary was a career official rather than a political appointee, Gore seemed to think that his signature would legitimize the endeavor.

The DOJ sent this so-called Gary Letter to Ross in December 2017. The letter claimed that a census citizenship question would help the government enforce the VRA by preventing the dilution of minority votes. Also, the letter relied on work by Ross's staff, not DOJ attorneys who enforced the VRA. And it was difficult to accept at face value given the fact that under Trump, the DOJ has not initiated a single VRA lawsuit. Ross didn't care. In a March 2018 memorandum, the secretary announced the addition of a citizen question to the 2020 census, relying on the Gary Letter to justify his action.

While Gore searched for a legal reason for the new question, the Census Bureau was entirely in the dark about the secretary's machinations. The Gary Letter came as a surprise to bureau officials, who had no idea that Ross had solicited it. They got to work gauging the impact of a citizenship question on the census—and the results were bleak. Census Bureau chief scientist John Abowd and his team of experts found that the question would "harm the quality of the census count" and require "very costly" follow-up procedures. Moreover, these experts noted that the government could *already obtain* accurate citizenship data from administrative records held by the Social Security Administration, the Internal Revenue Service, and other agencies. Adding a citizenship question to the census would generate "substantially less accurate citizenship data" than acquiring the information from these existing records.

There was another good reason for Ross to rely on these records: the law requires it. Congress has directed the secretary to use administrative records "to the maximum extent possible" instead of adding a question—any question—to the decennial census. Ross simply ignored this obligation.

The Census Bureau also calculated the precise harm that an altered census would impose on the data. Bureau experts compared response rates to the 2010 census (which had no citizenship question) and the 2010 American Community Survey (which did). They found that the drop in noncitizen response rate to the American Community Survey was 5.1 percent higher than the drop in citizen response rate. Using this data, they estimated that 5.1 percent of households with at least one noncitizen would refuse to answer a census that included a citizenship question. They later revised that estimate upward to 5.8 percent, then to 8 percent.

This plunge in response rate would translate into an undercount of 6.5 million people at a minimum. Immigrants and Hispanics, the bureau found, would be disproportionately undercounted. Undocumented immigrants are often afraid to state their legal status for fear that the Census Bureau might share it with other agencies, leading to their deportation. Lawful immigrants too may hesitate to declare their status for fear of being targeted or harassed by immigration officials. And citizens with immigrants in their household are frequently frightened to discuss the status of their noncitizen family members for the same reasons.

It is easy to gauge the consequences of such a dramatic undercount. Census data is used to draw districts for both state legislatures and the House of Representatives. Immigrants and Hispanics are more likely to live in urban centers, which lean left. If they are disproportionately excluded from the census, electoral power would shift away from America's cities toward its whiter rural regions. These areas lean Republican. Thus, state legislatures and the U.S. House of Representatives would be skewed toward the Republican Party for a decade. Immigrant-rich states such as California would almost certainly lose seats in the House.

A citizenship question would affect federal funding as well. Every year, the federal government provides about $800 billion to state and local governments for education, housing, health care, and other services. The federal government disburses much of this money on the basis of census data. An undercount would direct that funding away from diverse cities toward white rural areas that may not need it as much. Vital social services would be especially underfunded in immigrant and Hispanic communities.

In his memo Ross downplayed these dire repercussions, framing the data as inconclusive. "The Department of Commerce," he wrote, "is not able to determine definitively how inclusion of a citizenship question on the decennial census will impact responsiveness." Ross also provided no hint that he himself had asked Gore for the Gary Letter grounding the question in VRA enforcement. Ross merely relied on the letter as proof that the question would "permit more effective enforcement of the Act."

A coalition of voting rights advocates led by the American Civil Liberties Union, along with a group of state attorneys general, swiftly filed suit in New York, California, and Maryland. They alleged that the citizenship question was "arbitrary and capricious" in violation of the APA. U.S. district judge Jesse Furman, a Barack Obama nominee, heard the case in New York. Furman quickly faced a problem: it was apparent that he had not been handed all the facts. Typically, under the APA judges must limit their review to the "administrative record"— documents that decision makers and their staff considered, directly or indirectly, when contemplating a certain action. Early in litigation, however, Ross filed a supplemental memorandum in which he admitted that he had collaborated with the DOJ to justify the citizenship question. This memo essentially acknowledged that the administrative record initially provided to the court was incomplete.

In light of Ross's concession, Furman ordered him to complete the administrative record and authorized discovery beyond it. It is because of this extra-record discovery that we know the true story of the citizenship question's genesis. The plaintiffs uncovered a mountain of documents and e-mails that painted a complete picture of Ross's crusade for a citizenship question.

Finding evidence of "bad faith," Furman also let the plaintiffs depose Ross and Gore. In October 2018, the Supreme Court blocked the Ross deposition. At the same time the court allowed other extra-record discovery to continue, including the deposition of Gore. Justice Neil Gorsuch, joined by Justice Clarence Thomas, dissented, arguing that the court should "stay all extra-record discovery," including deposition. Gorsuch framed Ross's actions as nothing more than "cutting through red tape." Eleven days later, the Supreme Court refused to halt Furman's upcoming trial over the citizenship question. This time Gorsuch, Thomas, and Alito dissented.

Furman blocked the citizenship question in January 2019, issuing an exhaustive and acerbic 277-page opinion ruling that it violated the APA. Furman found that Ross's decision was arbitrary and capricious from top to bottom. In "a startling number of ways," he wrote, Ross's "explanations for his decision were unsupported by, or even counter to, the evidence before the agency." Ross rejected the Census Bureau's data based on his own subjective belief that it probably wasn't true. This speculation is "neither logical nor rational on its own terms," Furman wrote. It just "makes no sense." And by substituting his own conjecture for the evidence gathered by the bureau, Ross did not adhere to the law.

There was another reason, Furman wrote, why the citizenship question was illegal: "the evidence is clear that Secretary Ross's rationale was pretextual." Under the APA, a federal agency must clearly "disclose the basis" for its decisions. But "the real reason" for Ross's decision "was something other than the sole reason he put forward." Courts "have not hesitated to find that reliance on a pretextual justification violates the APA." And here Ross "decided to add the question for reasons entirely unrelated to VRA enforcement well before he persuaded DOJ to make its request." He and his aides also "sought to conceal aspects of the process" and overruled "near uniform opposition" from experts. Ross's pretextual falsehoods, Furman found, rendered the citizenship question unlawful.

Following Furman's ruling, the DOJ appealed directly to the Supreme Court. This stratagem was most unusual. In virtually every case, the losing party in district court must first appeal to the circuit court—here, the U.S. Court of Appeals for the Second Circuit. But the DOJ insisted that it could not take this intermediate step because the census forms had to finalized by June 30, 2019. The Supreme Court must hear the case as soon as possible, the DOJ claimed, so that the government could meet this strict deadline.

Complying with this abnormal request, the justices took the case and scheduled oral arguments for April. In the meantime two more federal judges—one in California and another in Maryland—blocked the question as well. Both judges found that it ran afoul of both the APA *and* the Constitution. (Furman found that the question only violated the APA.)

By the time the Supreme Court heard the case, the government was on a losing streak. As Solicitor General Noel Francisco strolled into the courtroom that morning, though, he did not look concerned. This court, after all, had upheld Trump's travel ban the previous term, despite a strong showing that it was motivated by pretext and bias. Once the administration coated that pretext with a veneer of legitimacy, allegedly conducting a "worldwide multi-agency review," the court's conservatives were willing to uphold it.

Similarly, in January 2019 the court's conservatives lifted two injunctions against Trump's ban on transgender military service. The president issued the policy in a 2017 tweet without consulting the Pentagon; by that point, transgender troops were already serving openly in the armed forces. A few weeks later Trump asked Secretary of Defense James Mattis to write a report that justified the policy on the grounds of national security. Four district courts found that Trump's ban was driven by unconstitutional animus toward transgender individuals. But after Mattis filed his report the Supreme Court allowed the ban to take effect, over the dissent of all four liberal justices. The majority did not issue an opinion, but it seemed that the five conservatives believed that the Mattis report provided sufficient pretext to justify the policy.

Why, Francisco might have wondered, would the census case be any different?

Oral arguments gave Francisco no reason to worry. As expected, the liberal justices tore into his defense of the citizenship question. "A lot of your argument[s] just do not appear" in Ross's explanation for his decision, Justice Elena Kagan told Francisco. And given that lawyers in the solicitor general's office "can come up with 60 pages of explanation for a decision—that's all post hoc rationalization—the question is, what did the secretary say? Where did he say it? When did he say it?" Kagan dismissed Ross's justifications as "conclusory" and "contrived."

Justice Sonia Sotomayor echoed Kagan's comment. "This seems like [Ross] thought of something," the justice said. She then channeled Ross: "'I want to add a citizenship question. I don't know why, but this is a solution in search of a problem. I've got to find a problem that fits what I want to do.'" And Justice Stephen Breyer cited Census Bureau expert John M. Abowd five times to drive home the point that all evidence suggested that a citizenship question would impair the "actual enumeration" of people in America.

Then New York solicitor general Barbara Underwood approached the lectern to argue against the citizenship question, and the Trump administration's fortunes turned. Chief Justice John Roberts asked why "it wouldn't help voting rights enforcement," since "citizen voting age population is the critical element of voting rights enforcement, and this is getting citizen information." Justice Brett Kavanaugh then told her that "the United Nations recommends that countries ask a citizenship question on the census. And a number of other countries do it. Spain, Germany, Canada, Australia, Ireland, Mexico ask a citizenship question."

"The question," Kavanaugh asked, "is, does that international practice, that U.N. [United Nations] recommendation . . . affect how we should look at the inclusion of a citizenship question in this case?" He called Ross's decision a "policy judgment" and asked why the court should halt it in light of conflicting "policy considerations." Justice Neil Gorsuch also pointed out that "virtually every English-speaking country and a great many others besides ask this question in their censuses."

Kavanaugh and Gorsuch's questions shocked many observers. Gorsuch has disclaimed reliance on international law and in his confirmation hearing proclaimed, "We have our own tradition and our own history. And I don't know why we would look to the experience of other countries rather than to our own when everybody else looks to us." In his opinions on the lower court, Kavanaugh has argued that international law and custom has virtually no role in the American legal system outside of treaties. Yet suddenly, both justices were looking to the "tradition" and "history" of other countries to shore up the citizenship question's legality. It seemed evident that Trump's nominees were eager to back the president—even if they had to rely on arguments they would normally spurn.

Alito too attempted to rationalize Ross's decision, questioning the validity of the Census Bureau's data. Roberts was tougher to read. Aside from his VRA question, he spoke little during oral arguments. And so, as the justices retreated behind the red curtain, it was hard to tell how the case would come out. Surely, the four liberals would vote to block the citizenship question, while Thomas, Alito, Gorsuch, and Kavanaugh would vote to uphold it. The case came down to Roberts, who did not show his cards.

Under normal circumstances, parties to a Supreme Court case have nothing to do after oral arguments but wait for a decision. These were not, it turned out, normal circumstances. Unbeknownst to the parties and the justices, as the census case made its way to the Supreme Court a separate drama was unspooling that centered around Hofeller, the longtime Republican gerrymandering master. And it had explosive implications for the challenge to the citizenship question.

Hofeller had a daughter named Stephanie who married a man named Peter Lizon in 2002. The two lived off the grid in West Virginia as self-described anarchists. By this point, Stephanie was already estranged from her father due to her disgust with his political work. She did not affiliate with Democrats, but she loathed Republicans and the gerrymanders her father drew to keep them in power. Lizon allegedly abused Stephanie, but domestic violence charges against him were dropped when Stephanie refused to cooperate with prosecutors. The couple had two children. According to Stephanie, her father threatened to challenge her custodial rights if she did not assist with the investigation into Lizon. When Stephanie still declined to cooperate, Hofeller allegedly accused her of child neglect and obtained custody of her first child. He then placed the child in foster care.

Due to this contentious relationship, Stephanie stopped speaking with her father. Hofeller died in August 2018. After Stephanie learned of his death, she visited her mother, Kathleen, and looked around the house for keepsakes. There Stephanie discovered four external hard drives and eighteen thumb drives. Hoping that they might contain old pictures of her and her children, she asked her mother if she could take them. Her mother said yes. That night as Stephanie looked over the files, she realized that the drives also contained materials pertaining to her father's work.

At the time, Stephanie was looking for a lawyer who could represent her mother in a legal proceeding—an attorney had filed a petition to have Kathleen declared incompetent, which did not succeed—and called Common Cause, a voting rights group, for a referral. As Stephanie later explained, she knew that the group would have no "allegiances" to her father and would recommend "actually independent counsel for my mother." While on the phone, she mentioned that she also had files relating to her father's work. Common Cause happened to be challenging North Carolina's legislative gerrymander in state court and recognized that the materials might be helpful. The organization issued a subpoena for the Hofeller files in February so it could take legal possession of them.

What Common Cause found was sensational. When advising Republican legislators and operatives, Hofeller stressed secrecy and data security. "E-mails are the tool of the devil," he told them. "The 'e' in email stands for 'eternal.'" Yet Hofeller had left behind 75,000 files involving the intimate details of his work across multiple states over the span of decades. Common Cause has only released a fraction of the Hofeller files, because North Carolina Republicans have alleged that the organization obtained them illegally. (So far, the courts have rejected this argument.)

In North Carolina, Common Cause is represented by the law firm Arnold & Porter. The same firm happens to represent several plaintiffs challenging the census citizenship question. When Arnold & Porter attorneys first reviewed the Hofeller files, they noticed something strange. In one study, Hofeller had written that adding a citizenship question to the census would create an electoral advantage for "Republicans and Non-Hispanic Whites." Recall that currently, legislative and congressional districts are drawn on the basis of total population. With census citizenship data, Hofeller explained, these districts could instead be drawn on the basis of "citizen voting age population" (CVAP). (The Supreme Court has never ruled on the constitutionality of drawing districts this way.) By counting CVAP instead of people, these maps "would clearly be a disadvantage for the Democrats," shifting representation toward white, rural, Republican regions. Using the Texas legislature as an example, Hofeller found that CVAP redistricting would drain representation from "Latino districts" and create more "GOP districts."

For this reason, Hofeller wrote, adding a citizenship question to the census would "provoke a high degree of resistance from Democrats and the major minority groups in the nation." But he had devised a neutral-sounding justification for the question: administration officials could claim that they needed citizenship data to better enforce the VRA.

As Arnold & Porter attorneys read these documents, they realized that Hofeller's words sounded familiar. That is because Neuman, the Ross adviser, copied them *verbatim* in the draft letter that he gave to Gore justifying the citizenship question on VRA grounds. Moreover, portions of Hofeller's 2015 study appeared in the Gary Letter, which Gore had ghostwritten.

Neuman had acknowledged that Hofeller gave him advice about the census but testified that he did *not* rely on Hofeller for "expertise on the Voting Rights Act." Metadata from the Hofeller files, though, indicate that Hofeller wrote up the VRA rationale at the exact time Neuman developed it: August 2017. A paragraph from Hofeller's write-up appeared word for word in Neuman's draft letter. And portions of Hofeller's CVAP study showed up in Gore's adaptation of the Neuman letter, which the DOJ sent to Ross.

The implication was disturbing: Hofeller had helped Neuman craft the VRA rationale, and his work formed the basis of the Garry Letter that the DOJ would ultimately send to Ross. Administration officials, then, must have known that as Hofeller demonstrated, a census citizenship question would benefit "Republicans and Non-Hispanic Whites" while diluting the votes of Hispanics.

On May 30, the plaintiffs submitted this evidence from the Hofeller files to Furman. They asked Furman to sanction Neuman and Gore for allegedly lying under oath to conceal Hofeller's involvement. But the plaintiffs had another aim: to call this new evidence to the attention of the Supreme Court. They filed a letter with the justices laying out the significance of Hofeller's previously concealed participation in the development of the citizenship question.

The DOJ responded to this filing with indignation, asserting that the plaintiffs had failed to draw a direct link between Hofeller and the Commerce Department. This defense fell apart on June 15, when the plaintiffs filed *more* materials from the Hofeller files with U.S. district judge George Hazel of Maryland. This evidence revealed that Christa Jones, chief of staff to Census Bureau deputy director Ron Jarmin, personally communicated with Hofeller, e-mailing him about the citizenship question. Jones played a key role in the creation of the citizenship question, so these e-mails seemed to disprove the administration's claims that nothing tied Hofeller directly to the manipulation of the census.

Throughout this flurry of filings, the Supreme Court did not respond directly to the new evidence. Nor did any justice refer to the Hofeller files when the court issued its decision on June 27, 2019. The ruling was incredibly complicated. While Roberts wrote the majority opinion, a different bloc of justices signed onto different sections.

At first glance, the ruling also looked like a victory for the government. Roberts devoted most of his opinion to swatting away challenges to the citizenship question. He wrote that the alteration would *not* violate the Constitution, because the government has "broad authority over the census" and may collect "demographic information" as it sees fit. He also found that the citizenship question was not "arbitrary and capricious" under the APA because Ross was permitted "to make policy choices within the range of reasonable options." The evidence before him "called for value-laden decisionmaking," and the court should not be "second-guessing the Secretary's weighing of risks and benefits." These sections were joined by Thomas, Alito, Gorsuch, and Kavanaugh.

Then in the very last section of his opinion, Roberts switched gears. Under the APA, he noted, an agency must "disclose the basis" of its action—the real reason, not a post hoc rationalization. The chief justice then described all the evidence that Ross had failed to fulfill this duty:

> The record shows that the Secretary began taking steps to reinstate a citizenship question about a week into his tenure, but it contains no hint that he was considering VRA enforcement in connection with that project. The Secretary's Director of Policy did not know why the Secretary wished to reinstate the question, but saw it as his task to "find the best rationale." The Director initially attempted to elicit requests for citizenship data from the Department of Homeland Security and DOJ's Executive Office for Immigration Review, neither of which is responsible for enforcing the VRA. After those attempts failed, he asked Commerce staff to look into whether the Secretary could reinstate the question without receiving a request from another agency. The possibility that DOJ's Civil Rights Division might be willing to request citizenship data for VRA enforcement purposes was proposed by Commerce staff along the way and eventually pursued.
>
> Even so, it was not until the Secretary contacted the Attorney General directly that DOJ's Civil Rights Division expressed interest in acquiring census-based citizenship data to better enforce the VRA. And even then, the record suggests that DOJ's interest was directed more to helping the Commerce Department

than to securing the data. The December 2017 letter from DOJ drew heavily on contributions from Commerce staff and advisors. Their influence may explain why the letter went beyond a simple entreaty for better citizenship data—what one might expect of a typical request from another agency—to a specific request that Commerce collect the data by means of reinstating a citizenship question on the census. Finally, after sending the letter, DOJ declined the Census Bureau's offer to discuss alternative ways to meet DOJ's stated need for improved citizenship data, further suggesting a lack of interest on DOJ's part.

"Altogether," Roberts concluded, "the evidence tells a story that does not match the explanation the Secretary gave for his decision." The "VRA enforcement rationale— the sole stated reason—seems to have been contrived," a mere "distraction." He ended with a swipe at the administration's clumsy lies: "If judicial review is to be more than an empty ritual, it must demand something better than the explanation offered for the action taken in this case."

This portion of Roberts's opinion—the most crucial part—was joined by Ginsburg, Breyer, Sotomayor, and Kagan. This bloc also dissented from Roberts's finding that the citizenship question was not "arbitrary and capricious." The conservative justices meanwhile dissented from Roberts's finding that Ross's rationale was unlawfully pretextual. They condemned Roberts for scrutinizing Ross's decision too closely, insisting that he had vast authority to alter the census as he saw fit. (It was surprising to hear these justices demand blind deference to Ross just one day after they *denounced* agency deference in *Kisor v. Wilkie*.)

The ruling was tough to decipher. It was not immediately clear whether Roberts had given the Trump administration an opportunity to fix its error. The chief justice had not found that a citizenship question was *inherently* unlawful. But if Ross's first justification was illegally "contrived," wouldn't a do-over be too? After all, a new justification would be *openly* contrived after the fact to shore up the question's legality. Moreover, the government had repeatedly told the courts, under oath, that it had to finalize the census forms by June 30. The government had used this deadline to rush the case up to the Supreme Court. Would the government now disclaim the June 30 deadline to keep fighting?

On July 2, DOJ attorneys told Hazel, the Maryland judge, that it had given up. The census forms, it announced, would be printed without a citizenship question. But the next morning, Trump tweeted that he was "absolutely moving forward" with the question, forcing DOJ lawyers to reverse themselves in court. In a humiliating hearing, DOJ attorney Joshua Gardner pleaded with Hazel not to accuse him of misleading the court.

"What I told the court yesterday was absolutely my best understanding of the state of affairs," Gardner told Hazel. "The tweet this morning was the first I had heard of the President's position on this issue, just like the plaintiffs and Your Honor. I do not have a deeper understanding of what that means at this juncture other than what the President has tweeted."

DOJ attorneys spent the Fourth of July holiday attempting to devise a new rationale. Then on July 5, Trump publicly declared that the "number one" reason for a citizenship question was "for districting." He had admitted the fact that his administration had worked so hard to hide. On July 5, the plaintiffs filed a motion with Furman identifying twelve separate occasions on which the DOJ stated, under oath, that it had to finalize the census forms by June 30. They asked Furman to "stop the Defendants' shenanigans" by enforcing the government's deadline and blocking the citizenship question once and for all.

On July 11 Trump abruptly announced defeat, ending the mad dash to prepare a new rationale and work around the June 30 deadline. He stated that instead he would order every federal agency to give the Commerce Department any records that might help the department measure the number of citizens and noncitizens in the country. (The president did not mention that this option had been available to him from the start.) After nearly two weeks of uncertainty—and more than two years of fighting—the battle was over. The administration had lost.

We may never know exactly what happened behind the scenes as the justices deliberated over the census case or whether the Hofeller files factored into Roberts's decision. Linda Greenhouse, *New York Times* veteran Supreme Court reporter, believes that Roberts changed his mind after first voting to uphold the citizenship question. "I've been obsessed with imagining whatever dark night of the soul preceded the chief justice's last-minute decision to shift course and reject the administration's position," Greenhouse wrote on July 3. "I readily admit that I have no sources for the claim I just made," she noted, but Roberts's opinion had "all the hallmarks of judicial tectonic plates that shifted late in the day to produce an outcome that none of the players anticipated at the start." She continued:

All four opinions scrupulously avoided any mention of what everybody knew: that documents brought to light in the weeks following the April 23 argument showed that the citizenship question was part of a plan not to help minority groups vote, but the opposite. The plan was to create and entrench Republican majorities in state legislatures.... If I'm right about the chief justice's late-in-the-day change of heart, did these revelations play a part, even a subconscious one? . . . Suffice it to say that it's hard to imagine the administration's litigating position undermined in a more devastating fashion.

It is indeed difficult to read Roberts's opinion without noticing a stark change in tone toward the end. Did Roberts originally write an opinion upholding the citizenship question and then, after reading the Hofeller files, tack on a final section blocking the question as illegally pretextual? If so, it would not be the first time he flipped his vote in a momentous case: the chief justice famously voted to strike down the Affordable Care Act's individual mandate, then changed his mind and upheld the mandate as a tax. We still do not know who leaked that information to the press. And no insider has yet come forward to substantiate Greenhouse's theory.

Whether or not the Hofeller files played a role in the Supreme Court's decision, they undoubtedly factored into the administration's admission of defeat. Hazel, the Maryland judge, reopened the case after reviewing the files, ruling that the new evidence "potentially connects the dots between a discriminatory purpose—diluting Hispanics' political power—and Secretary

Ross's decision." The judge planned to reopen discovery in the case, allowing the plaintiffs to gather more proof that the citizenship question was motivated by unconstitutional animus. Thus, if the Trump administration had not given up, it would have had to contend with a renewed investigation into Ross's fabrications. Dropping the citizenship question made this headache disappear.

In retrospect, it seems obvious that Roberts's opinion left no real room for Trump to revive the citizenship question. The chief justice appeared to be offended by the sloppiness of the government's cover-up. He knew—everyone knew—that the administration expected to win and that it was not particularly worried about submitting brazen lies to the court. That tactic had worked in the travel ban case; why wouldn't it work here?

The answer is that Ross and his allies left a wildly incriminating paper trail that rendered their rationalizations impossible to believe. They seemed confident that the court's conservative majority would accept their conspicuous falsehoods. But they miscalculated. Roberts would not debase and embarrass his court by feigning extreme gullibility. He would not sacrifice its prestige by giving credence to a blatant fiction. He would not, as he put it, "exhibit a naiveté from which ordinary citizens are free." Roberts's ruling in *Department of Commerce* reads like a warning to the Trump administration. It can be summed up in four words: Lie better next time.

As Joan Biskupic reveals in her new biography, *The Chief*, Roberts can be a political animal. He has a gift for triangulating, pushing the law as far to the right as possible without seriously risking the court's legitimacy. On the post-Kennedy court in high-profile political cases such as *Department of Commerce,* the big question is where Roberts will draw the line. The chief justice does not recoil at the notion of entrenching Republican power through 2030. He does not look down on a Republican administration using executive powers to further the current party platform. But when that administration cannot even put forth a remotely plausible justification for its actions, Roberts will flinch. He will flinch *not* because he opposes the underlying aims but instead because he recognizes that the public will view the court as a docile extension of the executive branch if it pretends to believe unbelievable lies.

Roberts takes seriously his role as the head of the federal judiciary. He does not want the country to see "Obama judges or Trump judges, Bush judges or Clinton judges." This desire may be naive, but it is genuine. The chief justice shares many goals with the Republican Party. But he does not want the U.S. Supreme Court to be seen as a rubber stamp for the Trump administration under his stewardship. *Department of Commerce* served as a reminder to the president and his associates that there are limits to the chief justice's partisanship and patience.

The Man in the Middle

O.T. 2018 ended as it began: on a note of uncertainty. In October 2018 as the justices filed onto the bench for the first day of arguments, they were missing a ninth member; Brett Kavanaugh was still fighting for his confirmation in the face of sexual assault allegations. In June 2019 as the justices filed off the bench after the last day of opinions, the final resolution of the census dispute remained in doubt. When the smoke finally cleared, it became evident that the Supreme Court had handed Donald Trump perhaps the biggest legal defeat of his presidency. The first term of the post–Anthony Kennedy court concluded as so many had before it: with a dramatic, hugely consequential 5–4 decision.

Yet something was different this time. When Kennedy voted with the liberals, he often swung far to the left. His decision in 2015's *Obergefell v. Hodges*, for example, announced a sweeping constitutional right for same-sex couples to marry—over the outraged dissents of the other four conservatives. Kennedy's departure in 2018 ended the era of the true swing vote—when a single justice

167

moved from one end of the ideological spectrum to the other—and took the court with him, ushering in the age of the Roberts Court and allowing the chief justice to assert control at last.

Unlike Kennedy, Roberts does not swing between extremes. He is a fundamentally conservative justice whose jurisprudence consistently aligns with the Republican Party. But he is not a hack or a reactionary. The chief justice is eager to push the law to the right, though he will inch toward the center when he believes that the court's legitimacy depends on it. Roberts's votes in *June Medical Services v. Gee* (the abortion case), *Trump v. East Bay Sanctuary Covenant* (the asylum case), and *Department of Commerce v. New York* (the census case) share a through line. In each instance, the chief justice voted to enforce legal limitations on the government's authority to carry out conservative policy goals. Roberts may share those goals; his broader jurisprudence evinces little sympathy for abortion access, immigrants, and voting rights. But if the government wants to achieve these aims, his votes imply, it has to do so the right way. There must be at least a veneer of legality and rationality for him to cite in upholding them.

Because Kavanaugh took Kennedy's seat, many observers expected him to fill his predecessor's shoes as the swing vote. It was not to be. Kavanaugh voted with the liberal justices in a 5-4 decision exactly once this term, in *Apple v. Pepper*—an important but not exactly monumental antitrust case. His opinion in *Flowers v. Mississippi* affirmed an important progressive precedent but broke little if any new ground. Otherwise, Kavanaugh served as a reliable conservative. He cast the crucial fifth vote locking partisan gerrymandering claims out of federal court. He signaled his determination to erode *Roe v. Wade* and its progeny. And he sided with the Trump administration in its brazen effort to manipulate the census in *Department of Commerce*, the clearest indication yet that he will run defense for the president who nominated him.

To the extent that Kennedy has a successor as a swing vote, it might just be Justice Neil Gorsuch. Make no mistake: Gorsuch is a rock-ribbed conservative who is no reliable friend to criminal defendants. He appears to see few constitutional restrictions on capital punishment— even when the execution may be torturous or the prisoner will be subject to religious discrimination in the death chamber. Moreover, Gorsuch's apparent rejection of *Gideon v. Wainwright* would leave millions of Americans without legal representation after they are charged with a crime.

Still, Gorsuch is willing to swing left on criminal justice when he believes that the original meaning of the U.S. Constitution requires it. His opinion in *United States v. Haymond*, affirming the right to a jury trial for certain offenders on supervised release, was Kennedy-esque in its wholehearted embrace of a far-reaching principle. Justice Samuel Alito responded by accusing him of writing a "dangerous" decision with "potentially revolutionary implications." Gorsuch's opinion in *United States v. Davis* too laid down a sweeping rule against unconstitutionally vague laws. Kavanaugh in turn charged his colleague of leading the court "off the constitutional cliff." When Roberts votes with the liberals, he writes carefully circumscribed and narrow opinions. When Gorsuch votes with the liberals, he goes for broke.

Justice Clarence Thomas meanwhile shored up his identity as the most conservative member of the court. Ironically, for a justice who rarely speaks from the bench, Thomas was also the most outspoken member of the conservative bloc in O.T. 2018. His separate opinions, especially in abortion cases, exude righteous energy and moral indignation. Thomas has never been one to fly solo; his lone concurrences and dissents are famed for their cavalier attitude toward precedent, prudence, and consensus. He will gladly go it alone when he believes that he alone is correct. But Thomas seemed newly invigorated this term. It is surely no coincidence that the justice spilled much ink lambasting adherence to precedent as soon as Kavanaugh replaced Kennedy. The conservative revolution that Thomas has long pined for may be nigh, and he will not let past progressive rulings stand in the way.

As the conservative justices begin demolishing precedent, Justice Elena Kagan stands athwart their bulldozer yelling "Stop." It is easy to envision an alternative world in which Kagan served as the chief justice, balancing her own liberal beliefs with the institutional imperatives of the court. She is not only a legal luminary but is also a strategic mastermind. Like Roberts, she is blessed with the gift of triangulation—or, less cynically, acuity and common sense. Her shrewd approach to the law helps her build bridges when compromise is feasible, as in *Kisor v. Wilkie* and *Madison v. Alabama*, when she nabbed the chief justice's votes. When Kagan cannot wrangle a compromise, she is unafraid to pummel the majority for failing to live up to its constitutional responsibilities. Her dissent in *Rucho v. Common Cause* crystallized the progressive vision of the

Supreme Court as a guardian of individual liberty against arbitrary, even malicious state power.

Opinion polls indicate that Justice Ruth Bader Ginsburg is the most widely recognized Supreme Court justice. She has become a feminist icon as "the Notorious RBG," a persona that depicts the justice as a tough-talking, take-no-prisoners liberal rock star. (Ginsburg is in reality soft-spoken, polite, and diminutive.) The moniker "Notorious RBG" was not as prominent when she fractured three ribs in November 2018, then underwent surgery for lung cancer in December. Ginsburg was as usual the fastest writer of the term, penning opinions in an average of just seventy-one days, according to Empirical SCOTUS's Adam Feldman. But she also had the fewest majority opinions—just six—due to her absence following surgery.

And so, in the 2019 term, Ginsburg "seemed to be handing the liberal torch" to Kagan, as National Public Radio's Nina Totenberg phrased it. As the most senior liberal justice, Ginsburg assigns the principal dissent when the court splits 5–4 along ideological lines. She gave the *Rucho* dissent to Kagan, a sign of her faith in Kagan's abilities. Roberts too plainly trusts Kagan to thread the needle: he assigned her the majority opinion in two cases, *Kisor* and *Madison*, in which he joined the liberals. As the shadow chief justice, Kagan can toggle between measured, centrist majority opinions and passionate, incandescent liberal dissents. She is the court's ultimate utility player.

The remaining justices—Alito, Stephen Breyer, and Sonia Sotomayor—played smaller roles this term. Each had their moments in the spotlight. Alito wrote the majority opinion in *American Legion v. American Humanist Association*, Breyer defended immigrants in *Nielsen v.*

Preap, and Sotomayor stood up for death row inmates in *Bucklew v. Precythe*. But overall, they played a less active role in a number of hot-button cases. This could change next term as a new set of blockbusters make their way to the court.

Already, O.T. 2019 is shaping up to be historic. The court will hear *Bostock v. Clayton County, R.G. & G.R. Harris Funeral Homes Inc. v. EEOC,* and *Altitude Express Inc. v. Zarda*—three cases asking whether existing civil rights law prohibits employment discrimination against LGBTQ people. In *New York State Rifle & Pistol Association Inc. v. New York*, the court will decide whether New York City can bar residents from transporting firearms outside their homes unless they are traveling to a nearby shooting range. The justices will hear *Mathena v. Malvo* to decide whether the Constitution requires a new sentence or parole hearing for juveniles who were sentenced to life without parole at a judge's discretion. Finally, the court will hear three cases, consolidated as *DHS v. Regents of the University of California*, that ask whether the Trump administration lawfully rescinded Deferred Action for Childhood Arrivals, commonly known as DACA, which defers deportation for 800,000 undocumented immigrants brought to the country as children.

And these are only the cases the court has already taken up. A slew of other blockbusters may join the court's docket next term—disputes involving the Affordable Care Act, transgender military service, same-sex adoption, religious liberty, contraception, and abortion access. The court could issue decisions in these cases around June 2020, in the middle of presidential campaign. In other words, the court would inject itself into a heated election. The next term may be the most explosive in recent memory.

Nineteen days after the court issued its final decisions of the 2019 term, Justice John Paul Stevens died at the age of ninety-nine. President Gerald Ford nominated Stevens in 1975, and he was confirmed by the Senate 98–0 less than one month later. Stevens served on the Supreme Court for thirty-five years and retired in 2010, when Kagan replaced him.

Stevens was a Republican nominated by a Republican president. Although Stevens's jurisprudence drifted leftward during his tenure, the justice continued to identify as a judicial conservative. His views were idiosyncratic; he championed free speech on the Internet but believed that states could ban the burning of an American flag. He supported the constitutionality of both campaign finance restrictions and voter ID laws. Stevens dissented in *Bush v. Gore* and extended legal protections to Guantánamo detainees over President George W. Bush's objections. Stevens advocated constitutional rights for same-sex couples and women seeking an abortion, yet he also voted to let the government treat unmarried mothers and fathers differently on the basis of sex.

To many Republicans, Stevens represented a missed opportunity. If Ford had appointed a more reliably conservative justice, the law would be much less liberal today. Stevens has joined the ranks of stealth liberals such as Earl Warren, William Brennan, Harry Blackmun, Sandra Day O'Connor, Anthony Kennedy, and David Souter—all justices appointed by Republican presidents who shifted leftward while on the bench. On the campaign trail Trump added Roberts to this category as well due to his decision upholding most of Obamacare.

Trump recognized during the 2016 election that he needed the support of white evangelical Protestants to win. He also knew that a key aim of this demographic was to abolish the constitutional right to abortion access. So, Trump partnered with the Federalist Society, a network of conservative lawyers led by Leonard Leo. The group helped Trump release a list of judges he would nominate to the Supreme Court. Once in office, Trump relied on the Federalist Society to select judges for the lower courts too, which he filled at a rapid pace. Leo hand-picked many of these nominees in addition to Gorsuch and Kavanaugh.

An unofficial rallying cry of the Federalist Society is "No More Souters." It wasn't just that Souter upheld abortion rights. Like Stevens, he also adopted a progressive stance on issues of great importance to Republicans: executive power, federalism, separation of church and state, campaign finance, gun restrictions, agency deference, gay equality, affirmative action—the list goes on. By asking Leo for help, Trump knew that he would nominate exclusively hard-line conservatives. The days of Republican presidents selecting independent-minded judges without a litmus test were over.

At Stevens's funeral in Arlington National Cemetery, Ginsburg praised the justice as a "model of independence" and "nonpartisan comity." Later she quoted William Shakespeare: "Take him for all in all, [we] shall not look upon his like again." There will indeed never be another Stevens—a Republican-appointed justice who charts his own course, building a pragmatic, distinctive jurisprudence that frequently clashes with Republican ideology. Kavanaugh will not be a Stevens or a Souter or even a Kennedy. Leonard Leo is too smart to have chosen another maverick.

Kavanaugh's staunch conservatism leaves Roberts as the man in the middle. The chief justice has inherited Kennedy's role as the Supreme Court's center of gravity. Roberts is not a traditional swing justice or a moderate; he is an institutionalist who balances his conservative jurisprudence with his desire to keep the judiciary above politics. As he goes, so goes the court. When it comes to the most contentious debates sundering the country today, the law of the land will be what John Roberts says it is.

Biographies of Current Justices of the Supreme Court

All biographies are derived from the U.S. Supreme Court website, https://www.supremecourt.gov/about/biographies.aspx.

Chief Justice

John G. Roberts Jr. was born in Buffalo, New York, on January 27, 1955. He married Jane Marie Sullivan in 1996, and they have two children—Josephine and Jack. He received an AB from Harvard College in 1976 and a JD from Harvard Law School in 1979. He served as a law clerk for Judge Henry J. Friendly of the U.S. Court of Appeals for the Second Circuit from 1979 to 1980 and as a law clerk for then associate justice William H. Rehnquist of the Supreme Court of the United States during the 1980 term. Roberts was special assistant to the attorney general, U.S. Department of Justice, from 1981 to 1982; associate counsel to President Ronald Reagan, White House Counsel's Office, from 1982 to 1986; and principal deputy solicitor general, U.S. Department of Justice, from 1989 to 1993. From 1986 to 1989 and 1993 to 2003, Roberts practiced law in Washington, D.C. He was appointed to the U.S. Court of Appeals for the District of Columbia Circuit in 2003. President George W. Bush nominated him as chief justice of the United States, and Roberts took his seat on September 29, 2005.

Associate Justices

All justices are listed in descending order of seniority.

Clarence Thomas was born in the Pinpoint community near Savannah, Georgia, on June 23, 1948. He attended Conception Seminary from 1967 to 1968 and received an AB, cum laude, from Holy Cross College in 1971 and a JD from Yale Law School in 1974. He was admitted to law practice in Missouri in 1974 and served as an assistant attorney general of Missouri, 1974–1977; as an attorney with the Monsanto Company, 1977–1979; and as a legislative assistant to Senator John Danforth, 1979–1981. From 1981 to 1982 Thomas served as assistant secretary for civil rights in the U.S. Department of Education, and he served as chairman of the U.S. Equal Employment Opportunity Commission from 1982 to 1990. From 1990 to 1991, he served as a judge on the U.S. Court of Appeals for the District of Columbia Circuit. President George H. W. Bush nominated him as an associate justice of the Supreme Court, and Thomas took his seat on October 23, 1991. He married Virginia Lamp on May 30, 1987, and has one child, Jamal Adeen, by a previous marriage.

Ruth Bader Ginsburg was born in Brooklyn, New York, on March 15, 1933. She married Martin D. Ginsburg in 1954 and has a daughter, Jane, and a son, James. Justice Ginsburg received her BA from Cornell University, attended Harvard Law School, and received her LLB from Columbia Law School. She served as a law clerk to the Honorable Edmund L. Palmieri, judge of the U.S. District Court for the Southern District of New York, from 1959 to 1961. From 1961 to 1963, she was a research associate and then associate director of the Columbia Law School Project on International Procedure. Ginsburg was a professor of law at Rutgers University School of Law from 1963 to 1972 and Columbia Law School from 1972 to 1980 and served as a fellow at the Center for Advanced Study in the Behavioral Sciences in Stanford, California, from 1977 to 1978. In 1971, she was instrumental in launching the Women's Rights Project of the American Civil Liberties Union (ACLU) and served as the ACLU's general counsel from 1973 to 1980 and on the National Board of Directors from 1974 to 1980. She was appointed a judge of the U.S. Court of Appeals for the District of Columbia Circuit in 1980. President Bill Clinton nominated Ginsburg as an associate justice of the Supreme Court, and she took her seat on August 10, 1993.

Stephen G. Breyer was born in San Francisco, California, on August 15, 1938. He married Joanna Hare in 1967 and has three children—Chloe, Nell, and Michael. Breyer received an AB from Stanford University; a BA from Magdalen College, Oxford; and an LLB from Harvard Law School. He served as a law clerk to Justice Arthur

Goldberg of the Supreme Court during the 1964 term; as a special assistant to the assistant U.S. attorney general for antitrust, 1965–1967; as an assistant special prosecutor of the Watergate Special Prosecution Force, 1973; as special counsel of the U.S. Senate Judiciary Committee, 1974–1975; and as chief counsel of the committee, 1979–1980. Breyer was an assistant professor, a professor of law, and a lecturer at Harvard Law School, 1967–1994; a professor at the Harvard University Kennedy School of Government, 1977–1980; and a visiting professor at the College of Law, Sydney, Australia, and at the University of Rome. From 1980 to 1990, he served as a judge of the U.S. Court of Appeals for the First Circuit, and he continued as its chief judge, 1990–1994. He also served as a member of the Judicial Conference of the United States, 1990–1994, and on the U.S. Sentencing Commission, 1985–1989. President Clinton nominated Breyer as an associate justice of the Supreme Court, and he took his seat on August 3, 1994.

Samuel A. Alito Jr. was born in Trenton, New Jersey, on April 1, 1950. He married Martha-Ann Bomgardner in 1985 and has two children—Philip and Laura. Alito served as a law clerk for Leonard I. Garth of the U.S. Court of Appeals for the Third Circuit from 1976 to 1977 and was assistant U.S. attorney, District of New Jersey, 1977–1981; assistant to the solicitor general, U.S. Department of Justice, 1981–1985; deputy assistant attorney general, U.S. Department of Justice, 1985–1987; and U.S. attorney, District of New Jersey, 1987–1990. He was appointed to the U.S. Court of Appeals for the Third Circuit in 1990. President George W. Bush nominated Alito as an associate justice of the Supreme Court, and he took his seat on January 31, 2006.

Sonia Sotomayor was born in Bronx, New York, on June 25, 1954. She earned a BA in 1976 from Princeton University, graduating summa cum laude and receiving the university's highest academic honor. In 1979 she earned a JD from Yale Law School, where she served as an editor of the *Yale Law Journal.* Sotomayor served as assistant district attorney in the New York County District Attorney's Office from 1979 to 1984. She then litigated international commercial matters in New York City at Pavia and Harcourt, where she served as an associate and then partner from 1984 to 1992. In 1991 President George H. W. Bush nominated her to the U.S. District Court, Southern District of New York, and she served in that role from 1992 to 1998. She served as a judge on the U.S. Court of Appeals for the Second Circuit from 1998 to 2009. President Barack Obama nominated Sotomayor as an associate justice of the Supreme Court on May 26, 2009, and she assumed this role on August 8, 2009.

Elena Kagan was born in New York, New York, on April 28, 1960. She received an AB from Princeton in 1981, an MPhil from Oxford in 1983, and a JD from Harvard Law School in 1986. She clerked for Judge Abner Mikva of the U.S. Court of Appeals for the District of Columbia Circuit from 1986 to 1987 and for Justice Thurgood Marshall of the U.S. Supreme Court during the 1987 term. After briefly practicing law at a Washington, D.C., law firm,

Kagan became a law professor, first at the University of Chicago Law School and later at Harvard Law School. She also served for four years in the Clinton administration as associate counsel to the president and then as deputy assistant to the president for domestic policy. Between 2003 and 2009, she served as the dean of Harvard Law School. In 2009, President Barack Obama nominated her as the solicitor general of the United States. On May 10, 2010, the president nominated Kagan as an associate justice of the Supreme Court, and she took her seat on August 7, 2010.

Neil M. Gorsuch was born in Denver, Colorado, on August 29, 1967. He and his wife, Louise, have two daughters. Gorsuch received a BA from Columbia University, a JD from Harvard Law School, and a DPhil from Oxford University. He served as a law clerk to Judge David B. Sentelle of the U.S. Court of Appeals for the District of Columbia Circuit and as a law clerk to Justice Byron White and Justice Anthony M. Kennedy of the U.S. Supreme Court. From 1995 to 2005 Gorsuch was in private practice, and from 2005 to 2006 he was principal deputy associate attorney general at the U.S. Department of Justice. He was appointed to the U.S. Court of Appeals for the Tenth Circuit in 2006. He served on the Standing Committee on Rules for Practice and Procedure of the U.S. Judicial Conference and as chairman of the Advisory Committee on Rules of Appellate Procedure. He taught at the University of Colorado Law School. President Donald J. Trump nominated Gorsuch as an associate justice of the Supreme Court, and he took his seat on April 10, 2017.

Brett M. Kavanaugh was born in Washington, D.C., on February 12, 1965. He married Ashley Estes in 2004, and they have two daughters—Margaret and Liza. Kavanaugh received a BA from Yale College in 1987 and a JD from Yale Law School in 1990. He served as a law clerk for Judge Walter Stapleton of the U.S. Court of Appeals for the Third Circuit, 1990–991; for Judge Alex Kozinski of the U.S. Court of Appeals for the Ninth Circuit, 1991–1992; and for Justice Anthony M. Kennedy of the U.S. Supreme Court during the 1993 term. In 1992–1993, Kavanaugh was an attorney in the Office of the Solicitor General of the United States. From 1994 to 1997 and for a period in 1998, he was associate counsel in the Office of Independent Counsel. He was a partner at a Washington, D.C., law firm from 1997 to 1998 and again from 1999 to 2001. From 2001 to 2003, he was associate counsel and then senior associate counsel to President George W. Bush. From 2003 to 2006, Kavanaugh was an assistant to the president and staff secretary in the Bush administration. Kavanaugh was appointed a judge of the U.S. Court of Appeals for the District of Columbia Circuit in 2006. President Donald J. Trump nominated Kavanaugh as an associate justice of the Supreme Court, and he took his seat on October 6, 2018.

Retired Justices

All justices are listed in order of retirement.

Sandra Day O'Connor, associate justice, was born in El Paso, Texas, on March 26, 1930. She married John Jay O'Connor III in 1952 and has three sons—Scott, Brian, and Jay. O'Connor received her BA and LLB from Stanford University. She served as deputy county attorney of San Mateo County, California, from 1952 to 1953 and as a civilian attorney for the Quartermaster Market Center, Frankfurt, Germany, from 1954 to 1957. From 1958 to 1960 she practiced law in Maryvale, Arizona, and served as assistant attorney general of Arizona from 1965 to 1969. O'Connor was appointed to the Arizona State Senate in 1969 and was subsequently reelected twice for two-year terms. In 1975 she was elected judge of the Maricopa County Superior Court and served until 1979, when she was appointed to the Arizona Court of Appeals. President Ronald Reagan nominated her as an associate justice of the Supreme Court, and she took her seat on September 25, 1981. Justice O'Connor retired from the Supreme Court on January 31, 2006.

David H. Souter, associate justice, was born in Melrose, Massachusetts, on September 17, 1939. He graduated from Harvard College, from which he received his AB. After two years as a Rhodes Scholar at Magdalen College, Oxford, Souter received an AB in jurisprudence from Oxford University and an MA in 1989. After receiving an LLB from Harvard Law School, he was an associate at Orr and Reno in Concord, New Hampshire, from 1966 to 1968, when he became an assistant attorney general of New Hampshire. In 1971 Souter became deputy attorney general and in 1976 attorney general of New Hampshire. In 1978 he was named an associate justice of the Superior Court of New Hampshire and was appointed to the Supreme Court of New Hampshire as an associate justice in 1983. Souter became a judge on the U.S. Court of Appeals for the First Circuit on May 25, 1990. President Bush nominated him as an associate justice of the U.S. Supreme Court, and he took his seat on October 9, 1990. Justice Souter retired from the Supreme Court on June 29, 2009.

Anthony M. Kennedy was born in Sacramento, California, on July 23, 1936. He married Mary Davis and has three children. Kennedy received his BA from Stanford University and the London School of Economics and his LLB from Harvard Law School. He was in private practice in San Francisco, California, from 1961 to 1963, as well as in Sacramento, California, from 1963 to 1975. From 1965 to 1988, he was a professor of constitutional law at the McGeorge School of Law, University of the Pacific. He has served in numerous positions during his career, including as a member of the California Army National Guard in 1961, on the board of the Federal Judicial Center from 1987 to 1988, and on two committees of the Judicial Conference of the United States: the Advisory Panel on Financial Disclosure Reports and Judicial Activities (subsequently renamed the Advisory Committee on Codes of Conduct) from 1979 to 1987 and the Committee on Pacific Territories from 1979 to 1990, which he chaired from 1982 to 1990. Kennedy was appointed to the U.S. Court of Appeals for the Ninth Circuit in 1975. President Reagan nominated him as an associate justice of the Supreme Court, and he took his seat on February 18, 1988. Justice Kennedy retired from the Supreme Court on July 31, 2018.

Acknowledgments

This book would not exist without Damon Linker, my exquisite editor. I am deeply grateful to Damon for trusting me to write this entry in the venerable American Justice series and expertly guiding me along the way. Thanks too to Garrett Epps, consulting editor of the series as well as a friend and a paragon of legal journalism. Garrett routinely helps me (and the rest of the world) better understand the U.S. Supreme Court.

The vast majority of this book is fresh material. Some passages, however, first appeared in articles published at *Slate*. I am grateful to *Slate* and our editor in chief, Jared Hohlt, for allowing me to adapt my work for this book. In addition, I am thankful for my *Slate* editors—Jeremy Stahl, Josh Levin, and Susan Matthews—who helped me develop my ideas about O.T. 2018 as it went along.

I would not be where I am today without Dahlia Lithwick, my friend, colleague, mentor, and so much more. Dahlia taught me everything I know about covering the Supreme Court, and she remains a constant source of joy and inspiration. I am eternally grateful for her support.

Finally, I am indebted to my family for more than I can possibly note here. My parents instilled in me a love for the law, for history, for writing, and for justice. My sister is my strongest and most loyal advocate. My husband encouraged me to make all the best decisions of my life and career so far. I owe this book to all of you.

Lightning Source UK Ltd.
Milton Keynes UK
UKHW022312290421
382884UK00010B/250/J